"FAST GROWTH THROUGH FUNDING

ISBN: 9798842577965

Imprint: Independently published

This book was produced in collaboration with Write Business Results Limited. For more information on their business book, blog and podcast services, please visit www.writebusinessresults.com or contact the team via info@writebusinessresults.com.

"*FAST* GROWTH THROUGH FUNDING

Entrepreneurs helping entrepreneurs achieve the extraordinary

An EHE Group Production

By Guy Remond, Gary Fletcher, Pete Evison, Ross Faith, Elliot Smith and Nyree Trimbel

ACKNOWLEDGEMENTS

The EHE (Entrepreneurs Help Entrepreneurs) team would like to acknowledge the brilliance, creativity and courageousness of the entrepreneurs we have had the pleasure of working with over the years. EHE would also like to acknowledge the smart, experienced investors who are prepared to back the vision of the entrepreneurs and their management teams. The beauty of business is the meeting of these great minds with a single purpose of providing value to the world.

DEDICATION

This book is dedicated to all the entrepreneurs, risk takers, creative minds, grafters and geniuses whose tenacity and drive make this world a better place.

CONTENTS

FOREWORD

by Carl Castledine

My first job, at the age of 15, was as a bingo caller. I spent time collecting glasses, working behind bars and in kitchens before I entered the corporate world and embarked on a career in the leisure sector, more specifically within UK holiday parks. I climbed the corporate ladder throughout my 20s and into my 30s and it was in my late 30s that I took a job at a business called Park Resorts, which changed everything.

This business was private equity backed and there was a real sense of entrepreneurialism within the company. During my time working there, it entered a period of change and this was when I realised that for too long I'd been an entrepreneur trapped in a corporate worker's body. I had become frustrated with the classic, bureaucratic-style PLC organisation, where you are empowered to do as you are told. Working in an environment where I was free to take some initiative made me realise I wanted to build a business for myself and bring some authenticity to the sector I had spent many years working in.

Armed with little more than an idea and a pitch deck, myself and two other co-founders set off for London with the aim of borrowing money from private equity investors in order to get our business off the ground. We were three very naive individuals, who were doing their best to become successful, and the experience of seeking investment in this setting was disarming to say the least.

We found ourselves in front of people who had a lot of experience of listening to pitches from "entrepreneurs like us", who were asking incredibly probing, and often technical, questions. I freely admit that we didn't initially approach this process with the rigour that the investors required. Fortunately, I had found my version of a Gary or Guy, who helped us formulate our pitch deck and gave us some very good advice. I can honestly say that without this person's input, we would not have received funding for our business. At that time, it would have been beyond my capability, knowledge and skill set to achieve that on my own.

Gary was introduced to me after we had received our investment. He was recommended by our private equity investor and he became Chairman of the business. Gary and I quickly formed a strong bond, because he recognised my entrepreneurial streak and helped me cultivate it. He recommended a coach to support my personal and professional development and introduced me to others in his business network. While Gary is no longer Chairman of my business, we have maintained a connection through our various business contacts.

What Gary helped me realise is that I had always been entrepreneurial – I think if your school reports say you're the kind of person who is a bit disruptive and gets easily distracted, you're probably an entrepreneur! One of the key differences between entrepreneurs and those who are better suited to corporate careers is that entrepreneurs tend to move to solutions more quickly and are good at finding different routes to those solutions. They like to cut through all the classic bureaucracy to achieve a result more quickly, and that's what this book will help you to do in relation to achieving fast growth through funding.

Enabling entrepreneurs to achieve fast growth

Too many people have amazing ideas that end up lost to the cutting room floor simply because they don't know where to take them next. What this book does, in a very concise and compassionate way, is provide an honest insight into the real journey of what those next steps could look like.

As I was reading it, I found myself grinning because I could relate to so much of what the EHE Group team were saying. It resonated with my own journey, both emotionally and practically, and you can tell that these are people who have been there, got the T-shirt and maybe picked up the odd scar along the way!

One of the reasons this book is so valuable to entrepreneurs seeking funding for fast growth is that it covers such a broad spectrum of funding types and explains when different types of funding are appropriate in different entrepreneurial journeys. The route I followed is just one of these options, and I found it enlightening to learn of other ways I could have approached funding for my business.

The Entrepreneur's Dictionary is a particularly useful resource, because it will strip away some of the jargon you will encounter on your journey to finding funding for your business and help you better understand some of the processes involved.

This book is a goldmine of information, regardless of what stage you are at on your entrepreneurial journey. The EHE Group was founded on the principle of entrepreneurs helping entrepreneurs, which is precisely what this book does so well. I have lost count of the number of conversations Gary and I have had over the years where we've wished we'd known something sooner or had someone who could demystify certain challenges that could have enabled us to accelerate the business' growth.

Entrepreneurialism is woven throughout the narrative of this book. It is a resource designed to enable entrepreneurs to cut through all the noise in the funding space and allow them to focus on what they do best; namely operating their businesses and making them successful so they can expand and provide solutions for even more people.

A note from the other side...

As someone who walked out of a well-paid corporate job into a startup that needed private equity seed funding to get off the ground, it would be fair to say I had a baptism of fire, but I wouldn't go back. With my two co-founders, we have created a business from scratch to one that is currently valued at £600 million.

I've always believed that any business should be driven by answering questions for three groups of people: customers, colleagues and shareholders/investors. I wanted to build a business that would honour all of these groups, and I'm proud to say that our first two employees are still with us, 15 years on, which is a testament to this approach.

We have been on quite a journey – our business employs over 2,000 people; we host holidays for over three-quarters of a million people every year; and our annual turnover is in excess of £200 million. But none of this would have happened if we hadn't had the courage to take our idea to investors, however frightening that might have been at the time!

The result is that all three of us still manage this business and we have taken many people with us on our journey. It has been an incredibly enriching experience to watch many of the people on our team evolve in their careers, as well as in their personal lives – the path we've followed has led to far more than just business success. There have been immense challenges along the way, but what we have created over the last 15 years is an incredibly resilient organisation that puts people at the heart of its decision making. By following some of the advice in this book (and perhaps by finding your own Guy, Gary or EHE Group), you too have the ability to put one foot in front of the other and accelerate your stroll down the entrepreneurial path into a run.

PREFACE

by Gordon Bateman

In 2018, I was talking to some investors in London who were finding it difficult to navigate the innovation landscapes outside of the city. I had also had similar conversations with entrepreneurs in the North West who were struggling to understand the investment landscape in London.

As someone who enjoys making connections, I invited several people from both of these groups for lunch. Luckily for me, many of them brought friends along with them and Investor Ladder was born. I had never run networking events before, and this was never about the event itself – it was all about making connections and encouraging conversations between entrepreneurs and investors.

Investor Ladder is now one of the largest networks of active equity investors in the science and technology field, with over 1,000 members around the world.

It's unsurprising, therefore, that when I met Guy and Gary we had something of a meeting of minds. We're all passionate about accelerating the growth of the innovation economy and collaborating was a natural fit.

In the years that I have been connecting investors with entrepreneurs, I've noticed one common theme from an investor's perspective that is often overlooked in the process of seeking investment for fast-growth businesses – investors want to get to know the entrepreneurs behind the business.

The events I run as part of Investor Ladder provide the perfect setting for these personal relationships to develop. This is crucial on your journey towards accessing funding to support your ambitions and business growth. As you'll discover when you move through the coming chapters, a slick pitch deck isn't enough to win investment.

In fact, one of the challenges facing both entrepreneurs and investors is the quantity of pitch decks and proposals that are submitted. I've spoken to investors who tell me they receive upwards of 900 proposals for every deal they are doing. That doesn't help either side because the good pitch decks can get lost in the noise.

Investors actively seek out the highest-quality investment opportunities — but as an entrepreneur you may not know how investors measure "quality" when they are looking at a business. This is why having experienced advisers, like the EHE team, to guide and support you on your journey to securing investment is essential.

One of the most important things to remember is that, as an entrepreneur, you are selling your business to prospective investors, rather than selling your product or service. Often entrepreneurs (understandably) get carried away talking about the products or services they provide, but this is just one small piece of the puzzle for an investor – they want to know about your whole business. They want to hear about who is in your management team, what operational processes you follow, and how you're increasing productivity, among other things.

Pitching for investment is a different ball game to pitching for new clients, and it takes a shift in your mindset to see your business through the eyes of a potential investor. This book will help you better understand what investors are looking for, but it also highlights the value of having an experienced and knowledgeable team supporting you as you seek the funds you need to propel your business to new heights.

Investors also want to know about you. As an entrepreneur, it is therefore hugely beneficial to connect with investors on a personal level, and to share your story, personality, and commitment to the journey you're on. On the other side, this is also a valuable opportunity to get to know the investor to see whether they are the right fit for your business because, as you'll realise as you read this book, not every investor will be the right fit for you and your organisation.

You are looking for someone who can be a great support vehicle for your fast-growth business, so vet potential investors to make sure they have the experience and knowledge you need, as well as values that align with you as an individual, and those of your business.

Investors, meanwhile, are looking for honest and transparent entrepreneurs. We all know there are risks involved in any business, but especially one that is targeting fast growth. Be honest about the risks you face, because a pitch deck that fails to acknowledge the risks ahead on your journey will look either wildly optimistic or under researched (or both!).

This again speaks to the importance of networking with potential investors and giving them an opportunity to see your passion and personality before you reach the official pitch stage. As an entrepreneur, you want to seek out investors who are willing to engage with you. You're looking for the investors who align with your values and understand what your business is about at every level.

Similarly, don't avoid mentioning your competitors, because this makes it appear that you haven't done your research. The bottom line is, include a healthy dose of realism in any pitch deck you put together or in any conversation you have about investment – as investors we don't expect anyone to have the perfect business opportunity and, in fact, if an investment looks too good to be true we'll be incredibly suspicious of it.

As I write this, the investment market is becoming increasingly competitive. There are more and more businesses seeking funding, but this demand from businesses has not been matched by increased funding from investors. This is why the quality of your pitch is so important and why it's vital you get the support you need as you embark on this process.

One thing that EHE (and this book) does really well is prepare entrepreneurs for their investment journey. Investors can't provide detailed feedback on every pitch deck, because they see so many of them. If you follow the steps laid out in this book, you'll be well on your way to having a strong pitch and the EHE team can further support you throughout the process. They won't just help you find investment, they will also ensure you, as the entrepreneur, are ready to receive investment.

Investment is about far more than the money – the last thing you want is an investor who disengages just as you need their support to overcome a challenge, or one who tries to offload their stake in your business at the first sign of a dip in performance. As you will know, business performance fluctuates and every company has problems of one kind or another. It's never entirely smooth sailing.

You're looking for an investor you trust and with whom you are comfortable being open and honest – you certainly don't need the added stress of an investor you're scared of breaking bad news to. You want someone who will be in the trenches with you when things do go wrong, because they undoubtedly will from time to time.

As you hit fast growth, you'll face new challenges in your business and this is when a strong relationship with your investor will really pay off, not to mention the need for good relationships with your wider network and stakeholders. All of these people have a role to play on your journey to fast growth.

As you'll learn in Chapter 6, there is no one-size-fits-all approach to seeking investment. There are many funding options available, and EHE can help guide you towards the one that's most appropriate for your circumstances.

This is why it's so important not to leave it too late to start thinking about your growth strategy and the role investment plays in that. If you wait until you need the money, you risk taking any investment you're offered, regardless of whether the investor themselves is a good fit for you and your business. This can have disastrous consequences, so I can't stress enough the importance of taking your time, having meaningful conversations with potential investors, and going about this process in the right way.

What you'll find in the coming chapters is an invaluable insight into how to have those conversations and what information you can prepare in advance to give you and your business the best chance of finding not only the investment you need, but also the right-fit investor for your fast-growth journey.

It's not as simple as finding an investor, delivering a pitch, and walking away with the funding you need – building these personal relationships takes time and is far more effective when it is facilitated by a team of professionals who not only know you and your business, but who also know a network of prospective investors. You can save yourself a great deal of time and energy by working with experts – like those at EHE – to connect with the right-fit investor for your organisation.

Building a business to raise investment is a different world from growing a business organically. To succeed at both, you need to bring those two worlds together and you need access to a wealth of expertise. Use this book as a starting point for your fast-growth journey, and then build the relationships you need to support yourself and your business as you travel down this road.

Gordon Bateman
Founder and CEO of Investor Ladder, and CEO of CRSI

INTRODUCTION

As an entrepreneur, the prospect of having a fast-growth business is exciting. We've been there and we remember the excitement of planning for that next stage of business development. The thought of seeing the company you've taken from its infancy through to stratospheric growth is thrilling. You know it's going to be something of a rollercoaster ride, and you can't wait to strap in. You're ready for the downs as well as the ups and you can't wait to get started on executing your big, bold strategy for growth.

There's just one problem though – your strategy requires funding, and funding at a faster rate than you can generate through your business alone. You need investment. Where do you turn? To your own savings? To friends and family? To the bank? To an equity investor? Even a private equity or venture capital firm? Do you crowdfund? Is there government funding available? There are many different places to source investment from, but when you're new to this side of the business world it can feel like a minefield. You're confident in your business and you know how to run it well, but when you start exploring investment, you feel out of your depth, alone and are suddenly aware of how much you don't know.

Believe us when we say we have all been there! Finding investors for your business can indeed be a minefield and navigating your way through it to the right investor or investment option for your business can be a challenge without a guide. We have written this book for exactly this reason, to provide you with a guide to the process of not only seeking investment, but also to explain the various business foundations you need to have in place to make that route to investment, and therefore fast growth, as smooth as possible.

When you enter the world of business investment, you'll hear a range of new terms and (if you're anything like we were earlier in our entrepreneurial journeys) will wonder what they all mean. The world of investment can appear overly complicated and a little overwhelming at times, but it doesn't need to be! Throughout the book, you'll find explanations of common terms that come up in investment discussions, and at the end of the book you'll find a glossary that explains not only the meanings of the terms themselves, but also what they mean for you as an entrepreneur. This is knowledge we've picked up on our own entrepreneurial journeys and we believe it's invaluable as you move your business towards fast growth.

We founded EHE Group because, as street-smart entrepreneurs, we recognised that there were very few places for people like us to go to find advice about seeking investment for our companies. We wanted to speak to people like us, who had been there, done it and got the T-shirt. That's why we set up our business, which helps entrepreneurs like you to connect with investors, helps investors find exciting investment opportunities from our community of forward-thinking entrepreneurs, and provides education, clarity and guidance along the way. This book is part of the education and guidance we offer, but we also have a podcast and helpful hints for investors and entrepreneurs alike on our website: https://www.ehe.capital/

What we realised from our own experiences of achieving fast growth in our businesses and sourcing the investment needed to make that happen, was that when you find the right investor the outcome is win-win. You get to realise your vision of running (and eventually exiting) a fast-growth and highly successful company and the investor sees the kinds of returns they are looking for, while being able to support innovative businesses to achieve more, in some cases even the extraordinary.

We have brought all of our collective experience, both as entrepreneurs and investors, together in this book. In Part 1, we explore mindset, which is one of the key components you need to get right to set your business on a fast-growth trajectory and to find the right investor for your company when the time comes. You may well already be working with a mentor or business coach to help you get your mindset right and put comprehensive business strategies for fast growth in place, in which case you are on the right track. If this is an area you haven't explored yet, this first part of the book will open your eyes to the essential role mindset plays in building a fast-growth business.

In Part 2, we look at the foundations that every business needs to have in place to successfully achieve fast growth with minimal friction: having the right management team in place and developing operational processes and systems to improve the business' efficiency and reduce its reliance on you, the entrepreneur. These two elements are also fundamental when it comes to seeking investment, so by laying these foundations in preparation for a fast-growth phase, you are also starting to become investor ready.

In Part 3 we explore what you need to do to ensure your business is as ready as possible to seek investment and we demystify the process. As an entrepreneur, when you are looking for investment for the first time you are generally at a disadvantage, because this whole process is new to you. Investors, on the other hand, have done this time and time again. We want to make you aware of what to expect and highlight some of the most common pitfalls entrepreneurs encounter during this process, to help you avoid at least some of the scars.

Finally, in Part 4 we'll look at how to develop your exit strategy, what you need to consider if you are thinking of selling your business and why this process isn't as different from seeking investment as you might think. We're also going to cover the future of investment and where we see the biggest opportunities for entrepreneurs in the coming years , as well as recessions and how you can ensure your business thrives in periods of economic uncertainty.

One thing to bear in mind as you read this book is that, very often, entrepreneurs and investors are presented in an "us and them" scenario. However, the truth is that when you are looking for an investor, what you're really looking for is a partner. Your investor should be someone who aligns with your business' values and who understands and supports your broader business goals. This is crucial and, when you find the right investor, it will make the whole process of not only attaining investment easier, but also accelerate your run towards fast growth.

This is why it's so important to ensure that your mindset and that of your team is in the right place. Having been on both sides of the table, we are also aware of how an entrepreneur's and an investor's mindsets can differ and where that may lead to friction if not managed correctly. Understanding both sides can help you build trusting relationships more quickly and effectively, which is why we're going to start by exploring the journey you've been on so far, the mindset you need as an entrepreneur aiming for fast growth, and how and why an investor's mindset will differ.

PART 1: MINDSET MATTERS

Before we start looking at the business itself and what you need in place to achieve fast growth, we're going to start by exploring the mindset you require if you're going to establish and lead a business that has the ability to achieve fast growth.

Without the right mindset, both for you as the entrepreneur and within your team, you will struggle to set your business on a fast-growth trajectory and you will also struggle to find investors who want to pour their money into your organisation. We can't stress enough how important having the right mindset is when it comes to seeking investment.

In the first two chapters, we're going to explore the journey of an entrepreneur who is on track for fast growth and what we mean by "fast growth". We'll also explain some of the crucial differences between an entrepreneur's mindset and the mindset of an investor. It's really important to understand these differences, because it will help you make sense of the funding process.

We'll also look at the key components of a fast-growth mindset and what steps you can take to cultivate this mindset within yourself (if you don't already have it), as well as within your core team. While the entrepreneur is the lynchpin of the business, you can't do everything alone, which is why it's so important that you have a strong team who share this fast-growth mindset if you are to set your business on a fast-growth trajectory and achieve everything you know you're capable of, and more.

Part 1: Mindset Matters

CHAPTER ONE
THE ENTREPRENEUR: FROM STARTUP TO FAST GROWTH

If you've picked up this book, chances are that you have already travelled a fair way along the entrepreneur's journey. You've spent time with your head down, focusing on growing the business that you're in. You're generating solid turnover and hopefully profit too. Over the years, you've employed some good people and some bad, but now you have a solid team in place. Broadly speaking, you have now reached a point where your business is working and it's growing. But you know it could grow faster and be more successful if you could access more capital.

Does this sound familiar? It's a very common challenge and one that we have encountered ourselves as entrepreneurs. We freely admit that we were very naive about the process of accessing more capital for our businesses the first time around. Who could blame us? The media seems to be full of stories about all the money that's "out there", ready for the taking by entrepreneurs, but the reality is that it's very difficult to not only find the money you need for your business, but also to find that money from the right organisation.

Whether you're looking for business angels or a friendly bank manager, we can tell you from our experience that they are hard to find. The whole process of finding and accessing the capital you need to grow your business faster is complicated and opaque. You will waste a huge amount of time on the hunt for this capital, which is time you don't have to spare, let alone waste, when you're running a growing business. This is why you're reading this book. Maybe you've already wasted time on the search for capital and are feeling disillusioned with the process. Maybe you are aware of your limited knowledge in this area and want to learn from entrepreneurs who have been there, done that and got the T-shirt. Or maybe you can see the huge potential your business has and want to find the quickest and most painless way to accelerate its growth. Maybe it's a combination of all of those!

One thing that all entrepreneurs at this stage will have in common is that both them and their business are ready for fast growth.

How to tell if you're on a fast-growth trajectory

There are four telltale signs that your business is ready to move into a period of fast growth. They are:

1. Your business is unique: it can't be the same as (or too similar to) an existing business because that won't attract investment. It has to be showing some level of success and it has to stand out.

2. Your business is growing: you need to demonstrate there is customer demand and there has to be evidence of growth, with the potential for fast growth.

3. Your business operates in a market that has potential; perhaps it is a growing market with huge potential, or perhaps it is a brand-new marketplace that you are trailblazing.

4. Your business is tech-led: this doesn't mean you need to have a tech product, but you as the entrepreneur have to be tech savvy and, at the very least, utilising technology to help you run and scale the business, if not using technology as your client-facing opportunity. It's not unrealistic to say that you are almost uninvestable if you're not tech savvy (and we'll explain what this means and why it's so important in the next chapter).

There is one slightly outlying scenario where you have a potentially fast-growth business but don't tick the boxes of being able to demonstrate growth, yet. This is where you need investment to develop your product or service before you begin trading. In this instance, you'll have a really solid business idea, intrinsically understand the market you're operating in and have a strong team in place. It's quite likely that you're a more experienced entrepreneur who understands what needs to be in place to go for fast growth from the get-go.

Defining "fast growth"

As entrepreneurs ourselves, we understand the desire to grow your business, and to grow it quickly. When we refer to fast growth within a business, the way we like to think of it is as "10x mindset". This means that you want to grow your business by 10 times its current size, rather than just see it double or even triple in size. Why is this important? In our experience, the mindset of entrepreneurs who want to go for fast growth is different to that of entrepreneurs who are content with incremental growth.

Strategising for 10x growth is different to strategising for incremental growth, where you might be aiming for just a five per cent year-on-year increase. You will need a strategy either way, but the kind of strategy you have in place for 10x growth will be different and it requires you, as the entrepreneur, to have a fast-growth mindset. Part of this strategy will cover how you fund 10x growth within your business and, just as importantly, who you source that funding from. It's also worth noting that 10x can refer to any number of the main KPIs and can be achieved over a period of time. The most important thing is that you are thinking with this 10x mindset from the get-go.

You need to find investors who match your mindset, because otherwise there will be tension in your relationship. For example, imagine your business is making a £50,000 profit and you need a finance director. You would likely employ a finance director who is used to dealing with smaller businesses and growth strategies. But what if you have the mindset where you're aiming for £5 million in profit in a very short space of time? That finance director with small-business experience won't be the right fit for your business. What you need is someone with more experience, who is equipped to deal with a bigger business. Someone with this level of experience will likely cost you more, although there are ways to pay a normal salary and offer a bonus paid on growth on exit. However, because you are both on the same page when it comes to the business' strategy and have a similar mindset, the relationship will be frictionless and they will support you in your goal to grow your company to that level. It's no different when you're looking for an investor. They also need to have the same fast-growth mindset as you.

We'll explore the fast-growth mindset in much greater detail in the next chapter.

The enthusiasm of entrepreneurs

As entrepreneurs ourselves, we know how easy it is to get swept up in ideas and race ahead with a business based on gut feel. Speaking generally, and from our experience, entrepreneurs are not normally financially oriented people.

People who are considered financially oriented are typically very logical, planned and structured. They won't embark on some of the seemingly crazy ideas that entrepreneurs will.

Entrepreneurs, who are largely not from financial backgrounds, are prepared to get their heads down and work to prove a concept or idea, even when all the logical people around them are telling them it's not going to work. The thing is, often entrepreneurs will make these seemingly crazy ideas work, and all of a sudden find themselves in a position where they need more money to continue to grow.

To illustrate the point of how differently entrepreneurs and finance professionals think, Gary likes to tell the story of his company, Forest Holidays. When he was developing this business, they spent £60,000 with one of the top four accountancy firms to provide a report on the concept for the business, which was to develop a network of holiday rental log cabins in woodlands and forests around the UK. The accountancy firm came back with the opinion that it absolutely wouldn't work as a business, because who would want to go on holiday in a forest in the UK in the middle of winter? That was in 2005. By 2009 Gary had a thriving business with nearly 100 per cent occupancy at all the UK forest sites all year round.

Entrepreneurs often talk about their "gut feel" and most will have a really strong gut feeling about what they're doing. They will have a gut feel they can solve a problem in the world, they will want to solve that problem and they have the drive and determination to work at it. This is often enough to get them going and to start seeing their idea come to fruition. However, it can only take them so far. They will almost invariably hit a point where they start thinking (and we've been there!), "This is working; this could really go somewhere... Now what do I do?!"

If you've reached this point on your entrepreneurial journey and are asking yourself this question, we're willing to bet that you've already started looking for answers. You have probably begun your search for funding and run into brick walls or closed doors. You've probably tried approaching friends and family to drum up some finance. One of them might have pointed you in the direction of an accountant, bank manager or maybe even a business angel. You've arranged a meeting, full of enthusiasm, only to leave feeling deflated after the person you met thoroughly burst your bubble by asking you questions you didn't know how to answer.

One of the challenges that you face as an entrepreneur at this stage of your journey, is the realisation that not everyone has the same deep-rooted belief in your ideas that you do. When you believe so strongly in what you're doing, it can be easy to assume that everyone else will just get it and that you'll have a queue of people who will want to invest. We're sorry to tell you that's not how it works!

Dealing with disappointment

This part of the entrepreneurial journey can certainly feel like an uphill battle. It is easy to get disheartened when you start looking for investment and are met with a lot of, "Nos", but you have to learn to love rejection. Investors will often give fairly spurious reasons for not wanting to get involved. These reasons might have nothing to do with you or your idea, it could simply just be bad timing, or that the investor doesn't want to get involved. Now that we are in a position to offer investment to entrepreneurs, we can see this side of the process and we know that our refusal to invest often says more about us and where we are currently than it does about the entrepreneur who has approached us or their idea. This is one of the reasons why we always give feedback to entrepreneurs and tell them why we have chosen not to invest on this occasion, and point them towards information that will help address the issue if that is appropriate.

However, as an entrepreneur on the receiving end of the "Nos" it can be very easy to become deflated very quickly. You have so much belief and passion for your idea that you can't understand why everyone else can't see its potential. You're met with a barrage of, "Nos" and you're going into meetings where people ask questions like, "What's your profit margin ratio of this, that and the other?", "How many years have you been in profit?", "How big is the market?",

"What's your EBITDA?" As entrepreneurs, we've had many meetings like this and, if we are being truly honest, have not always known the answers to all the questions being posed to us – or in some cases even what some of those terms even mean. As it turns out, many of these terms that sound complex are less complicated than you probably imagine and we'll be shining a light on their meaning throughout this book.

In all honesty, we still have meetings like this and still run into these issues, even though we have a lot more experience and knowledge of what we're walking into. The difficulties arise from the fact that entrepreneurs and investors typically have contrasting mindsets.

Getting these mindsets to marry up is the challenge. For example, Gary has two daughters who both work in the creative industry – one is a dancer and the other is an actress. He likes to describe this process of looking for funding as an entrepreneur as a similar process to attending an audition. His daughter might go to a dance audition and do the best performance she possibly can. It's flawless. But the producers are looking for a blonde dancer who's 5'2" and she is 5'6" with brown hair. At that point there's a mismatch between what she is and what the producers are looking for. In this scenario, it doesn't matter how good a dancer she is, because she simply isn't what they're looking for. Of course, she doesn't know that when she walks in for the audition.

This is the blunt end of investment and it's this kind of scenario that we want to help entrepreneurs avoid through our work at the EHE Group. Going to auditions like this is a waste of everyone's time, just like going to meetings with prospective investors who don't match your mindset is a waste of your and their time. Instead what you need to do is find investors with a similar mindset to you, because this not only reduces the risk of disappointment in the first place, but also means that once you receive investment your relationship will be much smoother.

However, investors often come at things from a very different perspective and with a very different mindset to entrepreneurs. This difference in mindset causes friction for both sides, especially when a "Rupert" gets in the mix.

Meet Rupert...

(Disclaimer: if your name is Rupert, please don't take offence! We simply use this persona as an example of some of the people you might meet on this journey who could be less than supportive – we're not implying this is true of all those named Rupert!)

Rupert is privately educated, very clever and graduated from one of the UK's top universities. He's financially trained, has likely worked as an auditor with one of the big four accountancy firms and has worked his way up through the ranks and into the world of private equity. Make no mistake, Rupert is the creme de la creme of accountants, but he has never run a business. He has never experienced any business hardships. He has never had to show the same level of grit and determination that an entrepreneur does. He is very smart from an accounting perspective, but has no practical experience of running a business.

Have you already met a Rupert (or maybe several) in your entrepreneurial journey? Gary certainly has. One particularly memorable encounter with a Rupert for him happened on Christmas Eve. A private equity firm, which had been following his company for a year and that was looking to invest a sizable sum in his business, held a meeting with him and his finance director. In that meeting, the accountant from the private equity firm presented Gary's business to him, based on figures from theoretical spreadsheets. Gary didn't recognise the business they were "showing" him. "It wasn't my business," he recalls. "I could see they'd done everything theoretically, but it wasn't that complicated on the ground. They just didn't understand how we did business."

Matching the mindset of an entrepreneur and an investor

The mindset of an investor is very often not aligned with the mindset and vision of an entrepreneur. When someone like "Rupert" is parachuted into the mix, with the purpose of "protecting" the investor's money, this can cause real problems and in some cases even prevent the business from developing in the way it should. This is because "Rupert" wants to run the business purely on figures, whereas the entrepreneur can see the bigger picture, knows where things could go and can see how their team could help them get there.

We aren't saying that there isn't a need for analysts to check certain elements of the business; they have a very important role to play. However, what you want to find is someone who has the humbleness and decency to ask the question in a polite way and seek to understand your perspective, rather than someone who won't be able to see that they (and their spreadsheet) could be wrong.

What it's important to understand is that the investor and the entrepreneur ultimately both want to end up at the same place (a profitable, fast-growth business), but they approach this goal from completely different ends of the telescope. The investor and their team want all the minute details, even when they can see it's a fantastic business with a great deal of potential. This slows everything down and, as an entrepreneur, is intensely frustrating. We're not going to lie, it's a painful process.

The good news is that, once the investment is in, the investor will tend to back off and that's when things really motor, the business achieves its growth targets and everybody wins. We know that there is light at the end of the tunnel because, as entrepreneurs, we have been through this process. The challenge for entrepreneurs who have never sought investment before is that you don't quite understand how frustrating this process can be, or how fragmented the investment market can be. This is why we're writing this book, to help you. We understand that entrepreneurs and investors approach things from completely different perspectives and, although they do meet in the middle and ultimately have the same aims, it can be a long and challenging process.

What you want as an entrepreneur and what we want to help you achieve (as both entrepreneurs and investors) is to find an investor who shares your mindset, which therefore makes this process a little less painful. Don't get us wrong, you will still have to answer questions to what will feel like an unnecessary level of detail, but when you know you both have the same underlying mindset it is much easier to work through this process.

This is why understanding your mindset as an entrepreneur is so important, because it will help you seek out investors who share your mindset. If you don't find someone with the same mindset as you, all that will happen is that you'll constantly butt heads. You don't want this relationship to be a struggle, where you're both pulling in different directions. You want a relationship where your investor supports you and shares their experience, without causing conflict.

This isn't about finding an investor who will agree with everything you say. We all need to be challenged from time to time and entrepreneurs can certainly have some wacky ideas on occasion and need to be brought back down to earth. However, you do need to have some common ground with one another.

It can actually be very interesting to look at the typical personality of an entrepreneur versus an investor from a scientific perspective. On the Myers-Briggs personality scale[1], an investor will typically be an S, which means they need to see all the logical facts before they can ratify the truth. An entrepreneur, on the other hand, is typically an N, which means they can project the future and vision. The simplest way to think of it is that those with a predominantly S personality type (investors) only

[1] https://mbtitraininginstitute.myersbriggs.org/

look backwards, whereas those with a predominantly N personality type (entrepreneurs) only look forwards. This is where the mismatch typically occurs, because the investor is looking for ratification for an idea, whereas the entrepreneur doesn't see the need for it.

Myers-Briggs isn't the only personality test that produces these kinds of results for investors and entrepreneurs, you can see a similar pattern in other systems as well.

Summary

If you can identify with the picture we have painted here, you're in the right place. As you move through this book, we'll be sharing our knowledge and experiences of the process of looking for funding from an entrepreneur's perspective. Our aim is to help you understand where best to look for funding, how to go about it, what you need in place in your business before you start the process and how to identify the right types of investors for your business.

We also want to share some of the pitfalls that you might fall down when you are new to this stage of the entrepreneurial journey. We have a few scars to share that will hopefully help you avoid falling into similar traps. What you'll also pick up as you work through this book is a strategy to help you navigate the funding process as an entrepreneur. It can be comforting to see what's around the corner and our hope is that by giving you some information about what's coming, you can create a more effective strategy.

In this first chapter we've looked at the difference between the mindset of the entrepreneur and the investor. What we'd like you to understand is that the investor has done this many times before. They are comfortable and they know what to expect. If we were to rate their preparedness for this process on a scale of 1-10, the investor is at about a nine. As an entrepreneur, we would estimate you're at about a four (if you're lucky) at the moment, but with our help and support, you can also be at a nine and meet the investor on a level playing field.

We've defined what we mean when we use the term "fast growth" and in the next chapter we're going to explore the mindset required for fast growth in much greater detail.

Fast-growth insights

EHE invested in Peppercorn, an insure-tech start-up, in 2022. This startup reinforced our philosophy of being flexible, as we hadn't envisaged investing in pre-revenue companies. However, Peppercorn had the mindset and foundations for fast growth. This started with an unbelievably experienced management team and operational expertise. They passed our diligence process and we even ended up increasing their funding requirement to robustly support the business.

This is a case of a company finding the right investor to provide the capital and support for fast growth.

Part 1: Mindset Matters

CHAPTER TWO
THE ENTREPRENEUR: FAST-GROWTH MNDSET

The first thing we'd like to make clear is that there isn't just one mindset for fast growth; there are a number of mindsets for fast growth. We talked in the first chapter about the 10x mindset and this is a concept we'll return to here, although it's important to be aware that 10x growth is not the ceiling, it's just the beginning. When you have a mindset for 10x growth, you could also achieve 20x, 50x or even 100x growth.

So, what are the mindsets for fast growth and what do they have in common? Guy and Gary have each developed a different mindset for fast growth. Guy's mindset for fast growth is in the context of the multiplier on your growth. Many companies are happy with five or 10 per cent growth. Guy freely admits he was happy with this level of growth when he started his first company. "I'd never run a business before," he explains. "That was what everyone else seemed to do and if you hit more than 10 per cent and got into the 20s, you were doing really well." However, if you are in this frame of mind and are aiming for five to 10 per cent growth, this is what you'll achieve.

Guy's turning point came when he joined the Strategic Coach® program and met Dan Sullivan, who introduced him to the concept of 10x thinking. "Quite frankly, I didn't believe it to begin with," Guy admits. "I thought, 'I can't possibly grow key parameters like revenue, net profit and number of people by 10 times, even over a number of years' – to my mind, that was impossible. However, what I came to realise is that the only reason I believed this was because it was all I ever used to do."

Dan Sullivan explained that the only difference between someone who has a 2x mindset and someone with a 10x mindset is their thinking and their strategies for achieving that growth. Guy adds that one of the points Dan stressed is that this level of growth doesn't need to happen in a year, or even two; it can take five, six, even 10 years. The timescale doesn't matter, what matters is focusing on developing a 10x mindset because this will affect the strategies you deploy.

What's more, when you start to deploy those strategies with bigger thinking, you'll achieve far more and do so much more quickly than you ever thought was possible. "It took me a while to get my head around that," Guy says, "But the proof is in the pudding and I can absolutely promise you it works. I did it."

Guy had an incremental mindset that he adjusted and changed, with the support of an experienced mentor and coach. Gary, on the other hand, has always been the sort of character who shoots for the moon. "Often that's unrealistic and it has caused me problems," he admits, "But I'm still doing it!" This too gets results, because it allows Gary to think on a 10x or more scale from the outset and this informs his strategies for business growth. What allows you to succeed with the approach of shooting for the moon is making those goals realistic, and the way you do this is by having the right strategies in place.

Whether you identify more with Guy or Gary in terms of your approach at this stage, the most important concept to grasp is that you become what you think about. Therefore, if you don't have a mindset for 10x or fast growth you are not going to become an entrepreneur or business who achieves that. Your mindset needs to be in the right place.

You might aim for 10x and only get 5x. That is what it is. But you may aim for 10x and get 20x. When we talk about how you employ and deploy capital in a fast-growth business, it is all about that focus on growth and the fundamentals.

Strategies to support the 10x mindset

It isn't only the mindset of the entrepreneur that's important. The mindset of the investor is equally key. What's interesting is when the investor has a 10x mindset, but the entrepreneur or their management team isn't quite there yet. In this scenario you will often find that the investor will over-invest (not what you were expecting us to say!) and they are happy to do so on the basis that you need to employ more sales people, improve your business' website, or get more support with your customer service. As an entrepreneur, that's often surprising because you are likely focusing on cutting costs rather than spending more. This is just one strategy you can deploy to help you fulfil that 10x mindset.

Strategy: Secure the right amount of investment, making sure you don't keep the amount so unrealistically tight that if one thing goes wrong you have to go back for more.

Spending money investing in yourself is one of the most important things you can do to support the development of a 10x mindset. Joining the Strategic Coach® program was the turning point for Guy (Gary is also a member of the program), who spent six years investing in his team before he invested in himself. "The biggest return I got on the business was when I invested in myself," Guy reveals. Joining the Strategic Coach® program not only encouraged Guy to think bigger, but also planted the seed that normal doesn't have to be small. It also gave him the confidence that thinking big didn't mean being unrealistic. In fact, it almost gave him permission to shoot for the stars.

Normal can be 10x growth or even 100x growth, but the point is you will deploy different strategies to get to that level, based around the likes of collaborations, when you open your mind and begin to think in this way. For many entrepreneurs, it's not that they can't think in this way, it's simply that they need someone to show them the art of what's possible. When this happens, your thinking changes and your mindset shifts up a notch. You have always had the ability to do this, you just needed a little push to get there.

Sometimes that push might even come from your investor. You might think you've experienced fast growth, but your investor wants even faster growth and is willing to do or invest X, Y and Z to make that happen. This is more likely to happen if you find the right investor with the right mindset, who really understands what you are trying to do with your business. When you're open to these possibilities and flexible in your approach, incredible things happen.

The key, however, is being prepared to invest in yourself and not just your team. Entrepreneurs have a tendency to put themselves last for everything, whether that's training, wages or time off. We're sure you identify with this and put your team and your business first. However, sometimes you need to put yourself first, because giving yourself an opportunity to develop and grow will have a profound effect on your business.

Putting yourself first also extends to your health, physical fitness and taking time off to recharge. We're talking about making time for exercise, eating properly, taking regular time off and having a mentor to support your professional development. This will help you develop the right mindset and, in turn, find the right growth strategies. Although being an entrepreneur can often mean making many sacrifices, make sure that you don't put yourself under so much personal financial dress that it affect your ability to focus on the business.

Remember, you are the lynchpin; you are the person who will drive this growth, motivate your team and show them what's possible and what the business can achieve if you all have the right mindsets.

Strategy: Invest in yourself so that you can learn and grow; be open minded in your approach.

When you start investing in yourself and your mindset shifts to 10x or more, you will be more conscious of the mindsets of those in your team, particularly in management positions. Once you learn about the impact mindset can have, it will often mean that the people you look to hire will likely be different to the ones you've employed before. You need to bring in people who genuinely believe it's possible to 10x or more the various multiples within your business. If you don't have the right people in place, they will get in the way and bring everyone else down.

When you start looking for the right people to join your business, you need to make sure you are fit, healthy, dynamic and that you have a growth mindset, because what you'll find when you start looking for different people to those you've already recruited to your business is that they will be interviewing *you*. The kinds of people you want to bring in will be interviewing you to see if you and your business are the right fit for them.

Gary recalls the interview he had with Jill, who joined his business to work in sales and marketing. "She absolutely interviewed me, no question," he states. "She wanted to know if I was the sort of person who could achieve that growth, which is why it's so important that you as the entrepreneur have the right mindset for growth."

Gary adds, "Jill became absolutely pivotal to the business and I know that if we hadn't recruited her, we probably wouldn't have been successful. It's as simple as that." He also reveals that the reason he interviewed Jill was because the person who was carrying out the sales and marketing at his business before simply couldn't get their head around the idea of 10x growth at the business. As a result, they had to move on because they couldn't see that it was possible to go from where the business was to where Gary wanted to be.

The concept of recruiting the right people, particularly to your senior team, is a topic we'll explore in much greater detail in the next chapter.

Strategy: *Focus on only recruiting people who share your mindset and can help you achieve your goals. To do this effectively, you need to get your mindset right first.*

The business is you

We've said several times that it's important to invest in yourself and put yourself first sometimes to develop the right mindset for fast growth, but it is also important to attract investors. From an investment perspective, the entrepreneur is very important in businesses up to the mid-market range (we're talking about a level of around £15 million EBITDA). In fact, the entrepreneur is disproportionately important in businesses up to this mark, because the whole culture of the business emanates from them.

> ### EBITDA (Earnings Before Interest, Taxes, Depreciation & Amortisation)
> A business' EBITDA is, essentially, a word for profit. It's a way for investors to standardise business valuations across industries and countries. Investors will often use a multiple of your EBITDA to calculate a value for your business, which will vary depending on the sector you operate in. When you start looking for investment, it's a term you'll hear a lot.

How does the level of involvement the entrepreneur has in the company affect the investment you're going to attract and whether investors will be interested in your business? It starts with the financial director or an accountant putting together the figures to go with your pitch deck. These figures look really ambitious, but you absolutely believe it is possible and clearly have the right mindset to achieve those figures. Those numbers haven't just been put on the spreadsheet to get the investment, they are there because you genuinely believe you can hit them.

As an investor, what you really want to hear from the entrepreneur is how they are going to achieve these projections. What are their fast-growth strategies? What is their fast-growth mindset that says they are going to achieve that? The answers an entrepreneur gives to those questions will show the investor whether they really believe in what's written down.

What investors really want to hear is that you are actually shooting for 15x or 20x growth, but for prudence the FD pulled this back to 10x. That's gold dust, but you have to be able to back up this assertion with the strategies you're putting in place to show that this is plausible. Without the entrepreneur at the helm, you lose this level of certainty and belief in the business' capacity for fast growth.

Dream, believe, learn, achieve

Gary likes to use the mantra: "Dream, believe, learn, achieve". "Believe" is the hardest part to get right, because you have to believe in yourself, and in your and your business' ability to achieve fast growth.

If you are getting stuck at the believe stage and are struggling to see how 10x growth could be possible in your business, we encourage you to look at the timescale you're giving yourself to achieve this in. You don't have to aim for 10x growth in a year or even two, it might well take longer than that. Allowing yourself to see 10x growth over a longer timescale will take the pressure off and make it feel more manageable. This creates a fundamental shift where you start to believe that it's possible.

Once you accept this fundamental shift, your strategies change. You might initially say you're aiming for 10x growth over five or seven years, because that sounds practical to you, but in reality you will likely achieve it in three years rather than five. Why? Because you believe it is possible, have changed your strategies to reflect that and are giving yourself and those around you permission to change your thinking.

The key is to simply practice doing it. If you notice one part of your business is growing quicker than another, ask how difficult it was and look at how you could apply similar strategies to other areas.

Getting to the belief stage is key, because this is when you will start looking for and finding alternative strategies. To give you a practical example, if you were looking to buy a house worth £150,000, your strategy for getting funding for the purchase would be very different than if you were looking to buy a house worth £500,000. It's the difference between being big and bold or being incremental and small.

Technology: a key piece of the puzzle for fast growth

We've already talked about the importance of technology in business today and the reason it's so important is that it's very scalable and it does help businesses to grow faster. For example, retailers no longer need bricks and mortar stores; they are able to scale up more quickly using the internet and a social media strategy.

Being tech-led is one of the keys to putting your business on a fast-growth trajectory and we would go so far as to say that any business that isn't tech-led won't survive the next 10 years. Remember, being tech-led is different to being a tech product company. When you are tech-led, it will make your business more competitive, either as a result of being able to generate higher turnover, higher profit or becoming more efficient.

It's only by looking at technology, understanding the technical side of your business and hiring the right person (or people) into your business from a tech perspective that you will be able to truly harness this to generate fast growth.

There are countless examples of how technology is allowing solo entrepreneurs and small businesses to compete with the big players. This is the age of the entrepreneur and it is technology that has levelled the playing field.

You might already engage with businesses that are effectively leveraging technology without necessarily realising it. For example, Guy doesn't buy his clothes from physical stores or the major retailers online. Instead, he looks for smaller, innovative companies that are producing clothes that really suit his lifestyle and way of thinking. These types of companies are often leading the way in terms of using new materials to offer different types of wardrobes.

"One such company I've discovered is Unbound Merino, which produces T-shirts and other garments from merino wool, but that feel just like normal T-shirts. However, their properties are different to traditional materials. Unbound Merino T-shirts are just as comfortable in warm weather as they are in cold; they are moisture wicking; they are antibacterial; they're comfortable and they are flexible. I found them through Facebook and it's a great example of how a small, innovative business can compete with much larger retailers," Guy says.

Adaptability: an essential trait

Adaptability is another essential trait that entrepreneurs require for a fast-growth mindset; you have to be able to deal with change and to do so quickly in a non-emotional way. The people in your team also need to be adaptable, because (as Peter Diamandis from the Abundance 360 Community frequently tells us) there will be more change in the next 10 years than there has been in the last 50 to 100 years.

Some people simply don't deal with change very well, but these aren't the kinds of people you want on your team when you're aiming for fast growth. The adaptability mindset is a key component of the fast-growth mindset and it's not only you who needs to have this, but all the members of your team too.

The tenacity mindset

Another key component of the fast-growth mindset is tenacity. This is about having the ability to deal with failure and the persistence to keep going and not give up when success doesn't come immediately. There are lessons in failures and what you need to do is accept when you get something wrong, learn from it, let it go and move on. If you are going to grow fast, it's almost guaranteed that one or two of your strategies will fail. You as the entrepreneur need to be prepared for this and you need to have a team around you who can deal with failure, find solutions and approach problems from different angles.

This ability to deal with failure will also serve you well when you're searching for investment because, as we've explained, you are very unlikely to secure finance on your first approach to an investor. It will often take multiple attempts and you will experience setbacks.

Investors view failure slightly differently, because they tend to be more risk averse than entrepreneurs. However, it's important to remember that what an investor is looking for is a proven track record of success in a similar industry. Smart investors recognise that there will be failures along the way and they don't worry about this as long as they can see that the entrepreneur has used those failures as learning points. What investors are looking at is how you and your team respond to failures and how you get over them.

The other side to this is that, if you don't fail occasionally, you're not taking enough risks in your business. To grow your business 10x, there are risks you are going to have to take. We are big believers in this.

Guy shares an example from his time at Cake Solutions. "At one point we thought it would be a good idea to open an office in Calcutta because our technical director had family there and wanted to be closer to them. It's well-known that employing tech people in India is considerably cheaper than the UK and we felt that, if our technical director was there, we could manage the quality." However, the reality was very different. "It never got off the ground, because there are 60 million tech people over there and finding good ones was near impossible. Eventually we gave it up as a bad job, wrote off the cost of the office space and moved on. We didn't consider offshoring ever again."

There is nothing wrong with trying something like this, because if you don't try you never know whether something will or won't work in practice. As Guy points out, if they hadn't failed in this way, the business probably wouldn't have succeeded in the way that it did. Sometimes you have to fail first to succeed later. However, there is a fine line between being tenacious and being stubborn.

As an entrepreneur you need to know when it's time to give something up as a bad idea and move on. There is no loss of dignity in doing that if you have the right team around you. The team shouldn't worry about this either. These decisions are the right thing to do, at the right time, and you made that decision for the right reasons. If it doesn't work out, you either change it and try again or you accept it isn't going to work and move onto the next idea. You need this kind of mindset and acceptance of failure to develop a fast-growth mindset.

One pitfall to watch out for here is when you, as the entrepreneur, aren't prepared to accept that your idea might not be working. Persisting because it was your idea and you are determined to make it work, regardless of whether that is realistic, is a negative mindset and not one that will result in fast growth for your business.

Summary

As you can see, many elements feed into a fast-growth mindset and you need to cultivate all of these if you not only want to experience fast growth within your business, but also if you want to demonstrate to investors that your company is on a fast-growth trajectory. When it comes to early stage businesses, almost all investors will be laser-focused on the entrepreneur and that means you also need to focus on yourself and your development.

If you are struggling to connect with the concept of thinking big and the fast-growth mindset, we would recommend the book *The Magic of Thinking Big* by David Schwartz to help you understand how to grow and change your mindset.

Being open-minded, adaptable, tenacious, accepting of failure and leveraging technology are all key components of a fast-growth mindset. You have to put yourself first and invest in your own development. You also need to look for people who share your mindset when you are recruiting and in the next chapter, we're going to explore how you can select the right management team to make your business more appealing to investors and to prepare it for fast growth.

Fast-growth insights

Many Entrepreneurs are not born with a 10x mindset. Guy Remond, one of the EHE founders, talks about this. His lightbulb moment came when he made the decision to work with an external coach, Dan Sullivan of Strategic Coach®, who is an entrepreneurial coach based in Toronto. Dan described how growing 10x is as easy as growing 2x with the right mindset.

Guy describes how he was sceptical about this to begin with. However, when he started to think 10x in all areas of his business (turnover, board appointments, net profit, operational thinking etc.) within five years he achieved this and more, and exited at a value far higher than he ever imagined could be possible five years prior.

PART 2:
THE BUSINESS-
STRONG FOUNDATIONS
FOR FAST GROWTH

Once you have your mindset in the right place for fast growth, there are a few areas that you need to focus on within your business to ensure it is ready for this fast-paced, transitional stage where things can and do change very quickly.

The first of these is ensuring that you have the right management team, who will be instrumental in propelling you towards fast growth and seeing you through this period. From an investor's perspective, the management team at a business is crucial, because they can make the difference between a business succeeding and failing.

As we'll explain in Chapter 3, building the right management team is all about making sure you have the right balance of skills and experience around the table. You have to be honest about what areas you might be lacking in so that you can find people who can fill those gaps. Being clear about your company culture and being able to communicate that effectively to both your existing team and anyone new coming in is equally crucial. You don't just want to hire people who have the skills and experience you need, but also people who are the right cultural fit because this will make your transition to fast growth much smoother.

The other foundational element for investment and fast growth is having operational processes and systems in place. Put simply, these not only ensure your company is well-run, but also demonstrate that it's well-run to any prospective investors or acquirers. We'll explore the kinds of systems and processes you need to put in place in more detail in Chapter 4.

First though, let's explore how to find the right management team to propel your business towards fast growth and make it attractive to investors.

Part 2: The Business –
Strong Foundations for Fast Growth

CHAPTER THREE
SELECTING THE RIGHT MANAGEMENT TEAM

If you're reading this book then you more than likely have a business and that means you will likely have a management team in place. The question you need to ask at this stage is whether they are the right management team to lead your business to fast growth. Some of them might be great at the startup level and do all the right things at this stage, but they may not have the skills necessary or desire to support the business on its fast-growth journey. In short, the people who got you from A to B are not necessarily the right ones to get you from B to C.

This doesn't necessarily mean you will need to let people go, it might be that you need to add to your management team to enhance it. The key is to recognise the weaknesses you have as a team and look at how best you can plug that gap.

Management team

A collection of senior personnel who set and execute the strategy, run and hold responsibility for the operations of a business. Basically they are those who are empowered to lead the business, who work together with the ultimate aim of making the business successful.

Enriching your management team

In small businesses, it's not uncommon to find people who are working across multiple areas of the business. For example, as the managing director you might also be working on sales and marketing. To move your company towards the fast-growth phase, you need to enrich your management team. That could mean bringing in a non-executive finance director, hiring a marketing specialist and introducing a dedicated salesperson. This will free you up, as the director, to direct the senior team and manage the business.

It's important to remember that the team is greater than the sum of its parts. Each member of the team is not only responsible for their own area of specialism, whether that's sales, finance, marketing or operations, but also has a role to play within the management team itself.

This differentiation in roles is important because the managing director should concentrate on directing and what you are aiming for is the management team to take away the day-to-day running of the business. This does two things; firstly, it enables you to think about growth and secondly, it enables you to focus on the due diligence and funding you need to achieve this fast growth when the time comes.

If you are still running the business in a day-to-day capacity when you're trying to raise funding or looking for buyers, something is going to give and that means at least one part of your business will suffer. This is why building the right management team is one of the foundations you need to enable and support fast growth. However, this process takes time, care and patience to do right.

Knowing when to relinquish control

In the early stages of a business, entrepreneurs can have a tendency to want to do everything themselves. This can make it difficult for them to relinquish control. However, if you want to put your business on a fast-growth trajectory, you need to recognise your specific Unique Ability® sooner rather than later and bring in people who can take on the aspects of running and managing a business that you are not as good at.

Understanding what you're good at

There are a number of tools you can use to help you work out what you're good at and therefore where you should focus most of your effort. The Strategic Coach® Program calls this your Unique Ability® and there is a specific exercise you can carry out to identify exactly what your Unique Ability® is, which you can find on the Strategic Coach® Program website: https://resources.strategiccoach.com/the-multiplier-mindset-blog/how-to-identify-your-unique-ability-with-these-6-tips

In some cases, what you're really good at might not be something you've recognised in the past. Taking the time to carry out this exercise will help you focus on what you're passionate about and good at and delegate the other tasks. This process also involves some acceptance on your part that, no matter how hard you work at certain things, they are never going to be what you're truly good at. What you're good at and what you focus on really doesn't matter as long as it fuels fast growth.

Being reluctant to relinquish trust and control is a barrier that you need to overcome if you want your business to grow quickly. There are two areas to focus on here. The first is simply trusting someone else to take on the managing and running of the elements of the business that are not your specialty, which is part of the mindset you need to develop for fast growth. The second is financial because at this stage you are likely investing quite heavily. To get a strong senior team in place, you need to pay them – whether that's through a salary, equity or a combination – and you will need to pay them a lot in comparison to what you have probably been used to. At the point at which you start doing that, you are probably not going to be utilising those team members fully because you are not at a fast-growth level yet. Remember you are investing for growth that you haven't yet achieved.

As an entrepreneur, it is therefore essential that you recognise what you are good at. More often than not, you are good at building a company rather than running a company. This is why it's vital that you bring in other people who can take over the running of the business, because otherwise when you hit the point of fast growth you will find you are putting more effort into running the business than you are into growing it. When that happens, the growth will stifle and slow.

By outsourcing the running of the business to a team you trust, you are freeing up your time and energy to allow you to focus on growing your business, maintaining a fast-growth trajectory and looking to the future to direct the business where you want it to go.

Why is your management team so important?

The senior management team is often an area that is overlooked in businesses in their early stages, but from an investment perspective two of the most important elements for investors are the entrepreneur and the team they have around them. An investor will look at this before they look at the size of the market, the financials of the business or anything else that they will need to dig into. One of the reasons for this is that a good management team can make a success of an average business, whereas a weak management team can make a failure of a good business.

When it comes to fundraising, regardless of where or who you are seeking funding from, the process from a prospective investor's point of view will be very similar and one of the first things they will do is look at the entrepreneur and their management team. If you don't pass this check, you are very unlikely to move onto the later stages of the process with that investor. In simple terms, you might have the best idea in the world but if you don't have the right team around you, you won't be investable.

What traits do you need for your management team?

With specific roles there will, naturally, be certain traits you look for, but there are some traits you will need in every member of your management team. Among the most important are good communication skills, being a team player, having high energy, being highly adaptable and getting things done.

In addition, you want people in your management team to be confident and feel able to challenge those around them and hold others accountable. This means you want people who have strong characters. This is also important because it won't always be smooth sailing in a business journey and things can (and do!) go wrong. There will be good and bad times within any management team, so you want to make sure that the people you have in these management roles can handle the ups and downs and that they can keep each other focused on and working towards the same goal.

There is no one-size-fits-all approach you can take for building your management team because every business is different. The key is to honestly assess the capabilities you have in your business and look at what gaps need to be filled.

For example, in the tech world it's quite common to see someone with great technical abilities in the chief technical officer (CTO) role, particularly in the early stages of the business. They have a fantastic idea, they've got it out of the gate and now they're ready for fast growth, but they are ultimately a technical person without much business experience. At this point, you would want to balance their technical skills with someone who has business acumen in the role of operations or sales director.

What skills you need in the various roles within your management team will depend on your abilities as the entrepreneur behind the business. If you're not sure where to begin, it's advisable to simply ask yourself what you are good at and what you are bad at, or what you don't enjoy doing in your business. If you can answer that question honestly, you will start to recognise what you're truly good at. Often this is what you'd prefer to spend your time doing.

However, many entrepreneurs will only spend around 20 per cent of their time doing what they love and are good at. When you're building your management team, you have to consider how you can delegate the tasks that take up 80 per cent of your time so that you can spend more of your day doing what you're really good at. Start by making a list of all the roles you would prefer not to do.

For example, if you've launched a marketing company you, as the CEO, might be a really good salesperson and marketer, so you will likely want to be heavily involved in deciding the sales and marketing strategies for the business because this is what you're good at.

EHE insight: Recruit people who are better than you. Some entrepreneurs can feel challenged by people who are better than them in a specific area and, as a result, they recruit those who they believe to be weaker than them. But what you need is people who are as strong, if not stronger, than you, particularly in your weakest areas.

Could a non-exec be the solution?

Recruiting people to your management team doesn't only have to mean bringing new team members in on a full-time basis. In fact, when your business is preparing for fast growth bringing people in as non-executive directors can be a good solution to give you access to the skills, experience and expertise you need.

Finding a non-exec who will question everything will help you prepare for the next stage in your business' journey. This relationship can be quite interesting, particularly in the first weeks and months, but it can be hugely beneficial. A non-exec can take a long, hard look at your company; they will more than likely make a tonne of suggestions and changes based on their own professional experience and this can significantly accelerate your company's progress.

A non-exec will not be full time and they won't be involved in the day-to-day running or management of the business. Their role is to be an adviser who works alongside all the members of the management team to coach, guide and advise them. This is very important because when you are part of the core internal team, it is easy to overlook areas for improvement or potential challenges that might be obvious to someone looking in from the outside.

Their focus might be to prepare the business for fast growth, or it could be that they have expertise in a specific industry that you lack in your management team. You have to ask whether the knowledge in your team is up to date and detailed enough to allow you to succeed in that industry. If it's not, introducing a non-exec can significantly accelerate your learning and therefore the progress and growth of your business.

Having a non-exec as part of your management team can also make your business more appealing to investors, because they will recognise that you have found someone to help provide the experience you lacked in a particular area.

Finding the right people for your management team

Understanding the gaps in your knowledge and where your strengths lie will define who you hire for your management team. This process can take time, but as an entrepreneur it's important to start thinking about this as soon as possible. You will more than likely have a good network of like-minded people, so start reaching out to them and lining people up in the background, before there is an urgent need to have someone in a particular role.

This doesn't have to be a direct approach to work for you initially. It could simply be that you recognise that someone has the skills you need and that they have the right mindset to fit into your business, so you keep in touch with them and make an approach when the time is right. It's important that you're sensitive in how you approach recruitment, particularly if one of the people you're interested in is either a client or works for one of your clients.

Entrepreneurs have to think ahead and start building a network of connections, regardless of whether they are planning to go for fast growth or seek external funding. If you are so busy running the company that you don't have time to attend events and keep up with your networking, the process of building the right management team will take much longer.

In our experience, the best way to build this network and find the right people is to talk about your aspirations for your business and your company culture with the people you interact with on a day-to-day basis – that might be suppliers or clients. This will often lead to deeper conversations that can help you get a feel for a person. If you think they might be a good fit for your business, make a mental note of what role you could see them in and then take the time to get to know them. We're not talking about poaching talent from other businesses. This is about having honest and open conversations and sometimes asking someone if an opportunity arose and the time was right, would they be interested in joining your business?

Taking this approach also allows you to see that person in action, particularly if they are working for a supplier or client. It means you have a much clearer idea of their strengths and abilities before you bring them into your business.

It's also important that you see the process of recruiting your management team as an investment, not a cost. Think of your business like a football team, which invests in its top players to help the team achieve on the pitch. This is how you need to think of your management team; you want everyone to be working towards achieving the long-term vision for the business, creating success and delivering shareholder value.

We talked earlier about recruiting people who are better than you, but an addition to that point is to recruit someone who is better than you think you need at this stage. You need to look to the future and think about who you will need in that role tomorrow, as well as today. Recruit people who are the best you can get at this stage in your journey.

Although there is no one-size-fits-all approach to building a management team, many companies follow a similar structure and route. Typically, the founder of the business will be the CEO and they normally recognise that the first person they need to support them is someone with a background in finance. We're generalising, but often entrepreneurs struggle to have a good grasp of the financial aspects of their business, which is why hiring someone to a financial director role is important early on.

Many entrepreneurs also look for a non-exec quite early in their journey. The non-exec is often instrumental in not only helping the entrepreneur become aware of the need to build a senior management team, but also in helping with recruitment. A non-exec can help you screen candidates and find the right people to join your management team. They will also have their own network, which can increase your reach and be incredibly valuable when you are recruiting for management positions.

When you are interviewing people to join your management team it's important that this is a collective decision, not one that is made only by the CEO. It's not only about finding someone with the right technical skills or expertise, but also a person who is a good cultural fit for the business. It is human instinct to hire people who are similar to you and who you would get along with, and while this is important, it's not the be all and end all. You want to hire people who will challenge you when necessary and who will enrich your ideas.

How to work effectively as a management team

The idea of having a management team who will challenge you and enrich your ideas is very important. You want your board to come up with good ideas for the business' development, but you also need to be able to condense and prioritise those ideas.

You might come up with 10 ideas and your management team's job is to vet those and condense the list to three that are worth exploring further. At this point, your finance director might say that you can only afford to do one of those three. This is when your operations director will step in and look at how you can improve the idea or make it more efficient. By following this process within your management team, you've taken a list of 10 ideas and condensed it to one really good and executable idea. Using your team's combined knowledge and experience, you will execute a project efficiently, quickly and properly. As an entrepreneur, this is what you are paying your management team for.

Each member of your management team is not only responsible for achieving their own goals, but also for working together to ensure their colleagues' and team's goals are achieved too. The example we shared above demonstrates how having the right management team in place can help your business operate more efficiently and allow you to focus on what you're good at.

This concept of collective decision making is particularly important, because it will help you make more balanced and considered decisions for your business, using all the facts available. You may well have a gut instinct about what to do – and you may decide to ignore the advice you're given and follow your instinct – but it's still important to listen to the input and perspectives of others.

Diversity within your management team is also important, and it's a topic that is being discussed increasingly in the business world. It is no longer a "nice to have", it's an essential component of a successful business in the 21st century. Diversity is incredibly valuable in a business setting and particularly at senior levels, because it ensures your ideas and decisions are enriched by perspectives from people from different cultures, of different ethnicities, of different genders and with different backgrounds and experiences. If you have a board made up of people who are from the same geographical location and who have similar backgrounds and experience, they will likely make similar decisions and see the world from a similar perspective. As soon as you introduce people who bring diversity in terms of culture, ethnicity, gender, disability, background and more, you get new perspectives that can challenge ideas and decisions in a very constructive way, ultimately leading to your business making better decisions.

Not only does diversity make your management team more balanced and result in more effective management for the company, it also makes your business a more attractive place to work and will therefore support recruitment. You will have a much broader pick of incredibly skilled people from a diverse talent pool than if you limit who you look to recruit by creating an exclusive, rather than an inclusive, culture in your business (even if you do so unintentionally). This is why it's so important to ensure you are not creating barriers for those in minority groups to enter and progress within your company.

Incentivising and rewarding your management team

As we mentioned earlier in this chapter, to get the best people in place in your management team you need to reward them appropriately. There are various ways in which to incentivise and reward those in your management team. If you are offering any performance-related package, this needs to be directly attributable to success, however that is defined.

Rewards can be in the form of pay, which would usually be linked to financial performance. However, another approach is to offer your management team share options in the business. In this case, more often than not you will be aiming for a successful exit from the business at some point in the future and you are therefore incentivising your management team to build shareholder value that will ultimately benefit them.

If you are considering offering share options, it's important that you consider the risks and challenges associated with this approach. When someone is given equity in your company and becomes a shareholder, you need to have a mechanism in place for the business to acquire those shares at an appropriate value should that individual leave the business. This will usually be covered through a legal agreement that includes terms and conditions to ensure that, should an individual leave, you do not end up with what's known as a rogue shareholder. We'll talk more about the mechanisms for achieving this in Chapter 6.

Rogue shareholder
A person who holds shares in your company and who will benefit from its future success, but who is not contributing to that future success or directly connected to the business.

You also need to think carefully about who you offer share options to. We recently came across a company that was seeking investment but that had a number of rogue shareholders because the business had given away equity without any agreement or mechanism to get those shares back when someone left. This particular business wanted to use half of the investors' money to tidy up these mistakes and get rid of their rogue shareholders. As an investor, the amount of money they were asking for and their valuation of the company didn't make sense as a result.

The lesson here is that if you want to offer share options in your business, make sure that firstly they are granted to the right people who will help deliver shareholder value and secondly that there is a mechanism in place to recover those shares and bring them back under control of the company should things go bad.

It's not all about the money

When you are recruiting your management team, particularly in the early stages of your business, the people you are approaching and trying to attract have to *want* to join your company. For them, it won't be all about the money and in some cases they will even be prepared to take a financial hit because they are enthused and excited about what you're doing. They want to take this opportunity and be part of the journey.

Everyone has bills to pay, but at this stage in your company's journey you're selling the dream. It's very unlikely that you are going to attract someone from a top-flight corporate with money alone – that person will need to want to join you and this will only happen if you can sell the opportunity to them.

Just as you would pitch your company to an investor, you can pitch it to potential members of your management team in the same way. What you don't want is to attract a team of mercenaries. People who are motivated solely by a high salary won't remain loyal and will leave your business as soon as someone else offers them more money.

Consider a hybrid approach

It is also worth noting that there are some roles that can be outsourced to external companies more easily than others and this can be a good option where either there isn't a need for someone to be full time internally or where you will struggle to afford the kind of people you need at the early stages of your business' journey.

One of the reasons businesses often seek investment is to enable them to expand their team, but it is worth being conscious that you can get external support in certain areas and this hybrid approach can be very effective. Among the business areas that are typically easier to outsource are HR, marketing and PR.

Summary

Having the right management team and support from the likes of non-execs is essential if you are aiming for fast growth in your business. Having a range of knowledge, skills and experience at a senior level in your company will help you make better, more balanced decisions and will make the whole business more efficient.

This is why building the right management team is one of the foundations for fast growth. Having the right people in place at a senior level will also make your business more appealing to investors, because it demonstrates that you are prepared for fast growth. The entrepreneur and the team is one of the first things an investor will look at and need to buy into, before they dig into the operational data (which we'll discuss in the next chapter).

As we've explained, there are various ways you can attract and incentivise your management team beyond salaries and it helps to think about how you will pitch your business to the right people by being clear about the opportunities available.

When it comes to finding the right people, the key is to identify what traits, skills and experience you need from your team and to talk openly about your company culture.

Fast-growth insights

The management team that you start with is not always the one that is suitable for fast growth. Gary describes one of many situations he has faced in building a management team suitable for fast growth. When Gary presented his 10x vision, one of his directors didn't believe this was possible and resigned. Gary then went to the market and aimed to find the best person in the UK for the role, someone who believed in the vision.

The net result was that Gary put a new management team in place with equity and was able to deliver on this vision in three years with a highly successful exit.

Part 2: The Business –
Strong Foundations for Fast Growth

CHAPTER FOUR
OPERATIONAL CONSIDERATIONS

For many entrepreneurs going through fast growth for the first time, it can be surprising how quickly it hits you and how unprepared you are – there are potential pitfalls in every area of a business and even if you think that you're prepared, you may still have some blind spots. In this chapter, we're going to talk you through some of the areas where it's easy to trip up. We're talking about areas that are essential for running a business, but not necessarily the most exciting elements. This covers everything from having solid HR practices in place to preparing regular management accounts and plenty more besides.

If you think about operational considerations before you are in the fast-growth phase or you have an experienced non-exec to guide you through the process, you'll be in a much stronger position than if you learn as you go and put together processes and systems while you're trying to achieve fast growth.

Operational considerations, in a nutshell, are lining all your ducks up. Any investor or acquirer ultimately wants to see that you have a well-run organisation, so that when they come in it will be relatively seamless from both an operational and a people point of view. Whether they are investing in your business or buying your business, they want to know that the organisation will run as normally and efficiently as possible, and therefore carry on the good work it has been doing.

When we talk about operational considerations, these span multiple areas of your organisation from HR and finance to project management. Below are just some of the things that an investor or acquirer will be looking at before choosing whether to invest in your business. This is far from an exhaustive list, but it will give you an indication of what you need to have in place.

HR

- Are your employment contracts up to date and representative of the current law?
- Do you have a staff manual/handbook and is it up to date?
- Do you have an online self-serve HR system containing everyone's details and is this information stored securely and accessible to only the people who need it?
- What are your salary levels? How often do you review them? Do you pay market rates, have you bought people in or are you paying over the odds?
- Do you have an induction programme?
- Do you have good staff retention rates – do you retain talent?

Finance

- Do you have reputable accountants?
- Do you have up-to-date monthly management accounts?
- Do you have up-to-date weekly cash flow reports?
- Does your accounting system plug into your bank and HMRC PAYE systems so that information can be pulled from the right places?

Project management

- If you're a technical company, do you have secure source code repositories?
- Do you have project management systems that run technical projects and operational projects? Is there one system for both, or different systems for different types of project?
- Do you have a time and attendance system for your team?
- Is there a company intranet or wiki available that shares useful information about your processes and systems?
- Are your relevant processes made easily available to new starters through your induction programme?

Board/senior team

- Do you have the right people on your board and senior team?
- Are the people on your board recognised names in your industry and do they have the experience required at this stage in your company's journey?
- Do you have the right people in the right teams across the organisation, not just at a senior level?
- Are the key people in your business willing to work with a new organisation for a period of time?
- Are there shareholders?
- Is there an EMI scheme in place?
- Is there a growth share scheme in place?

Company structure and tax

- Do you have a complex company structure that involves offshore accounts? Could that be construed as tax evasion?
- Are you up to date with all your tax payments in the UK, meaning there's no risk of HMRC coming after you for tax that should have been paid years ago?

A potential investor or acquirer will want the answers to all these questions (and many more). All of this data will then be assessed by various lawyers and specialists.

Ultimately, however, an investor or acquirer wants to see that a company is self-managing and doesn't rely solely on the existence of the CEO or founder. This becomes particularly important where an acquisition is concerned, because the acquirer will want to know they can extract the CEO without the risk of the company performance falling or the business failing.

The importance of building a Self-Managing Company®

Every entrepreneur that starts a company, and every startup business, has to think about how their company will become self-managing from the get-go. Focusing on becoming self-managing is how you build a competent team around you that supports what you're good at and helps you move away from what you're not good at.

As we said in the last chapter, as the founder you want to be working in the areas that you're good at, whether that's sales, marketing or product development. We explored the Strategic Coach® concept of Unique Ability® in the last chapter, but the point here in relation to creating a Self-Managing Company® is that you need to bring in people who support you in the areas you need help with. This is not only how you build a strong senior team that can help you take the company forward, but it's also how you lay the foundations for extracting yourself quickly from the organisation as an entrepreneur.

This is particularly crucial when it comes to your company being acquired, because there is generally a period following the acquisition, known as an earn-out, when you and your senior team will work for the acquiring organisation. In our experience, it is best if the entrepreneur can negotiate as short an exit from the business as possible. For example, when Guy sold Cake Solutions, he negotiated an 18-month earn-out, while the rest of his top team who were more important to the organisation had a four-year earn-out.

When you look at this from an operational perspective, the preparation for an exit from your company and the preparation for fast growth is the same in that your job as an entrepreneur is to set up processes, systems and tools that can carry your vision forward without you personally being involved in every aspect of the business. It's up to the leadership team, the directors and the shareholders to set up the "guardrails" through good processes and systems, and in doing so to enable everything to carry on.

We're talking about HR, sales, marketing, culture, finance; all these systems should be able to carry on as required without the direct interaction of the founder or the rest of the directors. When you reach this stage, you will have a self-managing company which in turn makes your business much more attractive to both investors and acquirers.

EHE insight: Conduct quarterly strategy reviews with your whole team. These are a platform for your entire team to understand what the company is doing, where it's going and why. These reviews get everyone on board, help align everyone around the core values of your company, remind everyone of your culture and highlight the performance of the business and any relevant strategies.

Embedding culture into processes

The processes at your business are important, but the processes themselves are just part of the picture. You also want to be in a position to demonstrate how you embed your company culture through your processes.

For example, a common question asked of entrepreneurs is, "How do you onboard teams and embed your culture?" You might respond, "When people start we run through X, Y, Z; we give them the staff handbook and we tell them what our culture is." However, this isn't a process that embeds culture. A process that embeds culture should be an ongoing learning process of that culture that is present on every step of an employee's journey. The systems and processes that you use at your business should all be intertwined with your company's culture.

This embedding of your company culture needs to happen not only with new employees, but also with any experts or senior people you bring in to support you as you prepare for and enter a period of fast growth with your business. What can sometimes happen is that these senior people may have their own ideas and historical ways of doing things that, if you're not careful, can change your overall culture and processes. When this happens, what you end up with is multiple systems and processes running in parallel and competing with one another.

Eventually, your company becomes unstuck by stealth. The lesson here is to ensure that you embed any non-execs, experts or advisers you introduce into your processes and culture in the right way. As we said in the previous chapter, you need people who challenge you and your way of thinking, but it's important that they buy into your culture and processes at a high level. If they don't buy into your culture and processes, they can end up challenging the very foundations of your company and that's counterproductive.

Measuring success

As well as looking at systems that help your business run more efficiently, it's also important to set up systems that enable anyone to measure the success of the business. For example, you want investors or acquirers to be able to see the efficiency and effectiveness of your sales team, as well as how they operate. This also brings benefits for you in terms of running the business, because it will enable you to scale that team much more effectively.

Let's say you have four salespeople doing £10 million, but another company in the same industry has ten salespeople doing £10 million, which is the most efficient? How can you measure performance to allow that comparison? One of the solutions is to set up key performance indicators (KPIs) because these allow you to demonstrate measurable success across different areas of your business, not only sales.

Sales is just one example and if your sales pipeline is likely to be a key attraction for investors or acquirers then you will rightly place a great deal of focus here because the due diligence in this area will be complex. However, the point is that investors and acquirers want to be able to look at your business and see clearly how you do what you do. Systems and processes allow you to clearly show how you work.

You have to think like an investor or acquirer. Ask yourself what they will want to look at; what KPIs will show an investor that you are performing well in every area of your business? Think about the data points that an investor or acquirer is most likely to zoom in on. Will it be staff retention, sales, conversion rates or renewals? All of these elements are measurable and you need to start measuring them through processes and systems as soon as you can, because these are the first things an investor or acquirer will focus on.

The questions you are asked will depend on why an investor or acquirer is looking at your business. If they are buying you for your talent, they will focus on staff retention, the contractual positions you have with your team and so on. If it's your subscribers, the focus will be on renewals, conversions and how much it costs to acquire each customer. If it's your sales pipeline, they will want to know about its history, how strong it is, what the conversion rate is, which markets you operate in, how large those are and so on. You want to have the answers to these questions easily available.

Management processes are equally important

You also need to look at the management processes you have in place and how your senior team works. When it comes to fast growth, attracting investment or a potential exit, it's essential that everyone on your senior team and board is rowing in the same direction. Meetings are important for your senior team, but no-one likes a meeting for the sake of a meeting, so you have to make sure that not only are your meetings productive and necessary but also that you can demonstrate their effectiveness to others outside your organisation.

There are certain meetings that you need to have regularly and that we would consider vital in the five years leading up to any investment or eventual acquisition. Regular board meetings fall under this category. These need to have an agenda and be minuted to ensure the proper process for board meetings is followed. Quarterly strategy reviews are also important so that you can demonstrate that the senior team are meeting every quarter, thinking about how the last quarter has gone, looking at whether the plan for the business needs adjusting and making sure everyone is clear on what the longer term plans are. These meetings should also have an agenda and minutes.

Then there are ad-hoc meetings that happen when you need to react quickly to a situation – the Covid-19 pandemic was a classic example of this. Businesses need to react quickly when situations like this arise and the beauty of being a smaller, more agile company is that you can react really quickly compared to much larger corporate organisations.

Again, however, these meetings need to have an agenda and be minuted.

Communication is key

Communication among the senior team is, of course, essential, but it's equally important that you communicate frequently and clearly with everyone on your teams.

Company updates are therefore important, particularly as your business grows its workforce. We would recommend holding these quarterly. During a company update, everyone in the business is present (either in person or virtually) and each member of the senior team will give an update on not only what has happened in the last three to six months, but also what is going to happen in the next three to 12 months. You can share highlights of what has been happening in the business and maybe discuss prospective clients who you are talking to. In our experience, this helps keep everyone interested in the company.

It is also good to share high-level figures, particularly if you have hit or exceeded your financial targets as a business, because this motivates everyone. Let's face it, we all like being part of a successful company.

Equally, if things aren't going as well as you had expected, it's important to be honest and tell your team that. That means if you have a bad quarter, you share that information, explain why you had a bad quarter and talk about what you are going to do to ensure the situation improves. You also want to make these company updates interactive. If you are facing challenges, ask the people on your teams for their input, because they may have ideas you haven't considered.

Making the management team approachable is key and this needs to be baked into your company culture. Everyone who works for you should feel as though they are able to approach the management team and that their ideas will be listened to when they do.

In addition to hosting these regular company update meetings, you can also send out a monthly newsletter to your staff, sharing the highlights of what has happened in the last month and what is coming up.

All of the minutes from your meetings and the communications you send out can go into a datary for an investor or acquirer when the time comes and this kind of information will help demonstrate that you have a high-functioning, well-run organisation.

EHE insight: Get these processes in place before you need them. When you only have a small team, it's much easier to communicate with everyone and share what's happening across the business. However, as your team grows that will become more challenging. If you have processes for these regular strategy meetings in place before you hit fast growth, they will just slot into what you're doing, but if you wait until you're in a period of fast growth before you try to introduce processes like this, you'll find they are an unwelcome distraction for some of the core members of your team.

This tip doesn't only apply to meetings and communication, but to all the processes across your business. If you wait until the point that you need them, you've waited too long. For example, if you wait until you have 70 employees before you sort out an HR system, you're going to waste an inordinate amount of time setting it up and putting it in place when you should instead be focusing on delivering fast growth within your business. This will distract you as the entrepreneur and your senior team away from the exciting journey that is fast growth.

How to start building processes for your business

Depending on the stage your company is at, you may not have many (if any) formal processes in place yet. The sooner you can start to create processes and systems the better, because this will make it much easier for you to target fast growth.

A good place to start is by mapping your customer journey and using this as a framework for your processes. Look at how you attract customers, how you nurture them and how you resell or upsell to them. Then you can build all the operational elements of your business around the customer and the product.

Pete explains that the project delivery process they created at Cake Solutions is something the whole team was particularly proud of and also a key element of what made the business so attractive to acquirers. "We created an end-to-end project delivery platform that started with how we onboarded a customer, moved into how we delivered the project for that customer and how we nurtured them, right through to how we marketed to them.

We were very proud of this process and our clients loved it, but it served an important operational function in that when we followed this process, reporting was easy because we were all reporting off the same data points. It also allowed everyone to see exactly what stage each project was at and it helped us identify opportunities within each project. Just as importantly, it embedded the culture we built at Cake not only in the business itself, but in our clients' journeys as well."

The result was that many of Cake's clients chose to adopt the Cake process themselves, which created opportunities within the business for spin-off services around embedding the company's culture and processes in other organisations.

Cake is a good example of a business where processes were instrumental in the success of the company. Pete has talked about the project delivery process, but this is far from the only area that had a strong process behind it at the company. Hiring and recruitment was another area where Cake had a strong process, as was marketing, building partnerships with both clients and technical partners, and even being active within technical communities relevant to the business. What made Cake stand out wasn't just the processes, but how transparent the business was about those processes and how much it was willing to share.

The shop front, if you like, was not only attractive but also representative of how the business was actually run. One trap that some companies fall into is that they create an incredibly attractive shop front, but once the due diligence from an investor or acquirer is underway it becomes apparent that this shop front doesn't represent how the company works behind the scenes.

What you have to remember is that lawyers for the other side (in this case the investor or acquirer) will always want to find issues for a couple of reasons. The first is because their client needs to know about these issues before deciding whether to follow through with an investment or acquisition. The second is to make sure that their offer is at the right level. On the surface, your ducks might all be lined up and looking serene, but if they see their feet paddling furiously to keep up when they look beneath the surface, they'll either pull out or they will chip you. Actively looking for problems within an organisation to use as leverage to reduce the offer is a really common practice.

However, you might be six or even eight months into this whole process by the time they uncover those issues, by which point you have emotionally bought into the outcome and this can be very challenging for entrepreneurs.

Ultimately, if an acquirer or investor discovers issues with your processes that mean the business isn't as well run as it first appeared, they are well within their rights to pull out of the deal altogether or to reduce their offer. This is why getting your operational processes and systems lined up is so important; it could literally cost you millions if you don't.

How to make sure you get your processes right

The way to make sure you get your processes and systems right is to start thinking about an exit, regardless of whether this is what you want at this stage. Ideally, have your eye on that goal as soon as you start your company, because then you will make sure things are done properly and that the right systems are introduced at the right time.

This is really hard and you won't get it right every single time, but we can tell you from experience that the more you think about this and the closer you get to having all the right processes and systems in place, the less work you will need to do when the time comes and the more likely you are to be in a good situation to get the best value you can from the company when you decide to exit.

If your business is performing well and growing organically without the kinds of systems and processes in place that we've discussed in this chapter, you can't just continue as you are. If you want to get investment or are aiming to be acquired, you need to start thinking about introducing processes and systems and you will need to invest in them.

In some cases you will be investing in systems that you might not need now, but that you will need in six or 12 months' time. If you want to go for fast growth and come out of it stronger, you need to take that leap and spend some money. These aren't just "nice to haves", they are essential foundations to support fast growth.

When you're looking at how you can leverage technology to support your processes and systems, it's important that you focus on two attributes in particular: being cost efficient and being scalable. What you want to avoid is buying a system today that needs to be upgraded in 12 months' time when you're halfway up your hockey stick of growth. You are looking for something that can scale with you without you needing to worry about it.

When it comes to investing in technology, such as customer relationship management (CRM) systems or HR systems, you will typically be looking at systems that offer a pay-as-you-go model based upon the size of your company. However, you always have to keep one eye on the future to make sure what you buy now is effective once you hit fast growth. For example, if you invest in a CRM system when you have 2,000 clients, take a close look at the payment structure and work out what will happen if you reach 10,000 clients, which is your target for your phase of fast growth.

Another tip is not to get carried away with features. Realistically you will probably only use about 30 per cent of any system, so work out exactly what you need and make sure you're investing in technology that delivers that so you're not paying for features you don't want or require.

EHE insight: Whiteboard all your processes with your senior team and whoever else you need from within the business. Map out everything from your customer onboarding process to your HR process. Drawing it out will arm you with the information you need to explore the market and find the right services for your business. Whether you will outsource or buy software as a service, you need to know precisely what problem you are trying to solve.

What you need from systems and technology will vary from company to company. Following this process and using a whiteboard to map out every process in your business will help you gain clarity over what you need in your business. Don't buy things because they look shiny and exciting; otherwise you'll end up spending more money than you need to and you could end up overcomplicating your business. Don't be afraid of outsourcing either, because this can be an effective way of managing some processes within your business.

For example, Cake outsourced its HR, finance and legal functions and that never changed, even when the company reached turnover of £10-11 million and a team of 60 to 70 people. However, it's important to look at your business and decide where you need to deploy the money and the power versus where you just need to record, manage and process things.

Operationalising a company is a process and the tools simply help you with that process. Before you get bogged down in deciding which tools to use, take some time to work out what is at the centre of your company. For most companies that will likely be the customer. From there you can map out all the processes you have in place and this will allow you to see where you have any gaps and work out what you actually need. Without this overview, it's very easy to become blinded by the systems and technology on the market.

What comes first, investment or processes?

While we have described operational processes and systems as foundational for fast growth, you don't necessarily need everything we've discussed in this chapter in place before you seek investment. In some cases, the investment you receive could be put towards hiring ahead or putting systems in place that you didn't have the funds or people to implement previously. However, an investor will want to see that your company is well run to give them confidence that their investment will be used to support growth within the business.

As we said earlier in the book, investors will firstly look at the entrepreneur and whether they are credible. Then they will turn their attention to the team that entrepreneur has built around them to decide whether they can achieve the goals being discussed. Once an investor has bought into the entrepreneur and their team, they will then turn their attention to the idea and what the business wants to achieve and, finally, to the operations at the company.

So, while we believe strong processes and systems are foundational for fast growth, not having them in place yet doesn't have to prevent you from seeking investment. This is also when it's important to understand the different kinds of investment available, because what is required for each is different.

Angel investment: This can also involve investment from friends and family at the start of your business journey. At this stage, there is probably very little expectation that you have much beyond a good idea, a vision as to how it could roll out and a few good people to help you get started.

Series A, B and C funding: At this stage you're up and running and you will have more processes and systems in place. You won't be expected to have everything in place though, because this funding is designed to get the business ready for fast growth. We'll explore these funding options in greater detail in Chapter 6.

Business exit: At this point, for your own benefit more than anything, you want to have everything we've talked about nailed down. If you don't you'll either lose the offer for your business altogether, or the acquirer will chip you down to the extent that you won't receive what you thought you would. Some business acquisitions and the subsequent payout to the founder will be based on them working in the business for a period of time and achieving certain targets. So, if you set targets for the next four years and you have to stay to see them through, you could struggle to hit those targets if you don't have all the operational elements we've talked about in place.

One point we would like to make is that if you don't have all the operational processes and systems in place yet, it is very important that you can show any potential investors that you are aware of where your weaknesses are and that you plan to put some of the money you raise towards correcting them.

Summary

When it comes to setting your business up for fast growth, there are certain foundations you need in place but you have to balance being proactive in some areas with being reactive in others. When you build a business, many opportunities will come along that you didn't see coming and you have to be able to react to those. You will be able to jump on those opportunities if you have the correct setup and this is where the operational processes and systems we've talked about in this chapter become so important.

If you don't have those underlying operational functions in place, it will be much harder to capitalise on those opportunities when they arise. You need to be confident that you have the right systems in place to enable you to scale quickly because this will give you the best opportunity of delivering and seizing the moment.

Fast-growth insights

Guy explains that his first business, Cake Solutions, started as a lifestyle business but when it was time for fast growth, the way in which the business was run needed to become more professional. This involved building out the management team and bringing in a non-exec.

In addition to bringing in the right people, the other step Guy took was to introduce systems that could support growth in the business. He acknowledges things didn't always go smoothly and that at times mistakes were made, but ultimately this gave the company a solid platform for growth and, once Cake Solutions hit fast growth, it was ready to fly and seize opportunities very quickly.

PART 3:
THE BUSINESS - GETTING INVESTOR READY

Getting your business ready for fast growth is also a great start for becoming investor ready. The foundations we discussed in the last two chapters will therefore prepare you well for seeking funding from investors. In this part of the book, we're going to explore the other core components you need to have in place to be attractive to prospective investors. We'll also discuss the processes involved in seeking investment and finding the right investor, starting with due diligence.

For entrepreneurs, the due diligence process can feel onerous, but it's crucial for both the investor and entrepreneur to ensure that their partnership is one that will work and benefit both of them in the long term. In essence it is an essential trust-building exercise. We'll also run through the funding options available to you as a business, explaining not only the different levels of investor but also alternative funding avenues, such as debt finance.

In Chapter 7, we take a deep dive into pitch decks and how to create a pitch deck that will capture an investor's attention and make them want to know more – an important element to get right when you're approaching investors.

Part 3: The Business –
Getting Investor Ready

CHAPTER FIVE
PREPARING THE
BUSINESS FOR
DUE DILIGENCE

Preparing for due diligence is a lot like having a relationship. In many ways you want to jump straight in and get married and in others you want to take your time in getting to know them. The majority of people take their time to get to know each other, ask questions, spend time together, stay over, move in, get to know each other's lives and maybe then get married.

The process of due diligence isn't that dissimilar, because it's leading to a partnership between an entrepreneur and company that is looking for investment and an investor who is looking to invest their funds and receive returns. Clearly an investor isn't going to hand over their cash on day one; they follow a rigorous and detailed audit process (due diligence) to evaluate an opportunity, identify key risks, develop mitigation plans and identify companies with fast-growth potential.

Due diligence can sound like a dry topic, but it's important to understand its purpose. For investors, the purpose of due diligence is to work out whether an investment makes sense. When you think about it, you spend your life carrying out your own due diligence in all kinds of situations.

Take a moment to think about due diligence from a personal point of view. Up until a certain age, your parents likely had at least some control or influence over the direction your life took. They will have given you skills that you hopefully took forward into your future, but then you reached an age when you started to explore what that future could hold. Would you go to university, take professional examinations or travel the world? When you're making decisions like this, you as an individual are doing your own due diligence in relation to what you want to become. You're evaluating your possible futures and deciding which one you want to work towards. This happens throughout our lives. We get presented with a great deal of information in life and we want to check whether it's correct and whether we're moving in the right direction.

It's a matter of trust

We want to get away from the idea that due diligence is a dry and onerous process and instead focus on what it's really all about: building trust. During due diligence, the entrepreneur and the investor will need to have open and honest conversations, which are incredibly important to the process. The investor needs to trust the information they are being provided with and the entrepreneur shouldn't feel as though they have anything to hide.

By taking a detailed look at the business, the investor will not only check the facts and figures relating to the business, but will also get to know the key people working in the company. When you view it as a relationship building exercise between the investor and your senior team, the process will likely feel less onerous.

People are generally the most powerful asset in any business; however in our experience a lot of businesses undervalue the power around the team. An investor needs to trust you and your team. They need to believe what you're telling them and trust that you are sharing what they need with them.

Your role in this process, as the entrepreneur seeking investment for your business, is to help the investor see where your business is going. This is a journey that you want them to join. Things will change along the way and you have to make sure your investor knows this and that they trust you to lead the way on that journey. They don't need to know about every tiny detail, but they do need to feel confident in the path you're charting and what checkpoints there are along the way.

While you can't know every turn in the road, you do need to know where you are heading. In a business, this destination is the broader business goals. The journey to achieving those goals might turn out to be different from how you currently imagine it, but you always know where you are heading and if you communicate this well, so will your investor. What you want to avoid is a sudden and dramatic change in direction. You don't want to tell people you're putting together an acapella singing group, only to change your mind and instead create a rock band that requires a drummer, bassist, electric guitarist and lead singer.

Entrepreneurs and investors need to be aligned and understand what their journey will look like, but they also need to be flexible enough to accept tweaks and shifts that happen along the way, as well as to embrace exciting opportunities that could arise. Building this relationship of mutual trust and understanding is an essential part of the due diligence process.

Due diligence works both ways

It's very easy to focus on due diligence as a one-way process, where an investor is assessing your business, but it's just as important for you as the entrepreneur to carry out your own due diligence on the people who are going to be investing in your business. You want to ensure that anyone investing in your business is a good fit and that they will potentially be able to bring more to the table than just money.

You need to understand how an investor will be involved in your business; are they the kind of investor who will just let you get on with things, or do they want to have constant oversight of what's happening? Coming back to the relationship analogy we shared at the beginning of the chapter, this is a partnership that has to work for both parties. Both of you need to say, "Yes."

As investors, we really like it when the entrepreneurs we are talking to have questions for us. We can gather a lot about their personality and professionalism from the questions they ask us, as well as from the answers they give to the questions we ask them.

The three stages of due diligence

There are three main stages to due diligence:

1. Evaluation
2. Investigation
3. Legal

Evaluation: This is the initial contact you make with a potential investor, who will carry out a light form of due diligence. This stage is to assess whether you are a good fit and for the investor to assess the opportunity before going further.

Investigation: This is where the investor determines the viability of the offering. It's a much more detailed process that will involve face-to-face meetings and information gathering on a greater scale. The investor will assess the management team, the size of the market, the USPs of the business and the problem that the business is solving. The investor is assessing whether the company has fast-growth potential.

Legal: At this point you have effectively agreed a deal in principle and you are moving onto a term sheet and a process of documentation gathering. This is typically the stage of due diligence that people dislike, however it's necessary because the information and answers gathered here will be warranted against in the final stages of the deal.

Stage #1: Evaluation

When you're preparing for the evaluation stage, less is more as a general rule. However, you don't want to be too brief. It is helpful to remember that what you want to achieve at this stage, through the likes of your pitch deck that we'll talk about in more detail in Chapter 7, is to capture the imagination of the investor. You want to get them interested in your business and your journey without going into too much detail – the finer detail comes in the investigation stage.

You want to hook the investor in the evaluation stage and it's only once you get to the investigation stage that you reel them in. The evaluation stage can feel a bit soulless, because you typically won't meet the investor face-to-face at this point. You'll be sharing a lot of information and documents (like your pitch deck) but you won't get a great deal back.

This is all about making the investor curious enough that they are prepared to give your business their full attention in the investigation stage, but what do you need to do that effectively? We believe you need the following to capture that initial interest from an investor:

- A strong pitch deck covering a host of areas (more on this in Chapter 7)
- A well-defined business plan and model
- To know what kind of investment you're looking for and why (more on this in Chapter 6)
- A well thought-out business growth plan
- A sensible valuation
- An exit plan

EHE insight: The exit plan is more important than you might think at this stage in the process, because investors want to know what kind of opportunity they are investing in. Is this an investment that will run for three, five or even 10 years? Or is it a "who knows?" opportunity?

Ultimately you want to put together a comprehensive pack that will allow someone outside of your organisation to assess the opportunity you're offering.

As Ross explains, a good pitch deck can even lead to new opportunities for your business. "One company that sent us a pitch deck really caught our imagination, because we could see three different types of value models within it. We were excited to start the investigation stage after recognising this and explore the more foundational elements of the business that could not only create more value for the entrepreneur, but also for us as investors if we collaborated."

Stage #2: Investigation

Once you have "hooked" your investor and captured their curiosity you need to get their full attention and this is where the investigation stage starts. The focus here is on what's called a viability review, where you go into much more depth than you do at the evaluation stage.

During the investigation stage, the investor will carry out much more rigorous questioning. This is also when your whole management team will start to have face-to-face meetings with the investor to assess all the areas of your business and all the key people in your business. When it comes to your people, an investor will want to assess their background, credibility and their previous successes and failures. An investor will also look at the digital footprint of both key individuals and the business itself at this stage.

There will be much more detailed investigation into the market you're operating in and the type of product or service you offer. One of the key questions an investor will have of your product or service is whether it's scalable. They will also carry out a thorough review of your financial projections, along with the supporting assumptions, review your historic financials and audit your strategy and growth plan. A simple way to look at it is that the evaluation stage sets the scene and the investigation stage provides a lot more of the fine detail behind the scene you have set. An investor wants to see that this detail supports that scene; that it matches the picture you've painted through your pitch deck.

Elliot shares an example to explain the kinds of detail investors will be looking at after the evaluation stage. "One company we looked at had lost £1.9 million in their first year and they weren't asking for any more funding. The obvious question to ask after identifying that loss was, 'how are you bridging that gap?' In this case, they had a letter of intent from a debt-based funder, but this wasn't immediately clear from what we received in their pitch deck."

Another key part of the investigation stage is sensitivity analysis. This is when your company's financial model is stress tested to allow for changes in different variables. It's a process of looking at the "what ifs", such as, "what if there is a reduction in the company's revenue?" This stage of questioning can be quite tough for an entrepreneur. However, it's important to understand why it's so important for an investor to carry out this kind of analysis. Investors don't want to have to put their hands in their pockets too quickly, so they want to know that an entrepreneur is prepared for all kinds of eventualities, including any they hadn't previously thought of.

There is a distinction between different phases of development and investment, and unexpected additional expenses. For example, if a business asks for an investment of £2 million for its first phase of development, the investor won't want the entrepreneur to come back to them three months in and say they miscalculated and that actually they need an additional £2 million. Carrying out a sensitivity analysis during the investigation stage helps avoid this kind of situation from arising.

EHE insight: Carry out a SWOT (strengths, weaknesses, opportunities and threats) analysis of your business. This process allows you to look inwards before then looking outwards and it can prepare you well for this stage of due diligence. Investors will often use a SWOT analysis to lead their approach to certain areas of due diligence, so carrying out your own SWOT analysis and sharing that can be very helpful. Don't neglect the weaknesses and threats of your SWOT analysis, because these are the elements investors are likely to ask the most questions about.

As an entrepreneur it can be tempting to only show investors the good side of your business, but they are just as interested (if not more so!) in what keeps you up at night and where they can potentially help and support the business to grow. Avoid thinking of this as an "us and them" scenario and instead view it as a collaboration. Remember you're building a relationship with your investor and that means you want to have openness and trust.

As investors, we want to be approachable to every entrepreneur we work with, so that if something does go wrong they feel they are able to knock on our door and ask for our advice. At the end of the day, we generally all have a common goal and that's to grow a business to a point where we can all have a successful exit at some point in the future.

In Chapter 4 we talked about professionalising your organisation from an operations perspective and much of what was discussed there will be explored in the investigation stage of due diligence. What you need to be aware of when it comes to due diligence is that you need all the data about your operations to be readily available and easy to find, as it will make the whole process much less stressful for you. This is about being professionally organised.

What often happens as you build a business is that you end up with some data in a hardcopy, some stored on email, some saved on one PC, something else saved on another PC or the cloud. Everything is scattered everywhere. Our advice is to bring everything together as soon as you can – it's never too early to create a centralised data room where you store all the key documents relating to the business. These include (but are definitely not limited to):

• Incorporation documents
• Shareholder agreements
• Copies of previous accounts
• Employment contracts and the CVs of all your key people

Data room
This is a web-based depository that contains all the important data about your company, from title deeds and leases to insurance details and agreements with suppliers.

Elliot remembers how useful this was from his experiences of helping Guy sell his business. "The potential acquirers sent an initial due diligence checklist as part of their viability review. I think they thought they were going to have to wait months to get all the information and we sent it all over to them within a week! They even got in touch to tell us they couldn't believe how quickly and professionally we responded. It added an air of professionalism to the business and it built trust and confidence very early in the process."

Investors will wait for a reasonable period of time, but they don't like to wait too long. They want quick answers and they want to see that, to the best of your abilities, you have already worked out what their questions will be. At the same time, however, don't be afraid to ask questions of the investor if there is something you don't understand.

If this is the first time you are seeking investment for a business there will be a lot you don't know and the investors won't expect you to know everything either. As we've said, it's important to be professionally organised and this extends to having someone who takes ownership of the due diligence process. It really helps to have one person in your business who gathers all your responses, as this avoids 10 people all doing the same thing, which not only wastes people's time but also has the potential to make the process confusing.

Stage #3: Legal

Once you complete the investigation stage, you will have agreed the deal in principle. You will then have heads of terms, which outline the key details of the investment and have been agreed by both you and the investor. Heads of terms isn't a legally binding document, but it's what you use as you move through this final stage of the process to formalise the agreement and create a legally binding document that both parties sign at the end.

If we return to our relationship analogy, by the end of the investigation stage you've got engaged and by the end of the legal stage you will be married. Heads of terms are a sign of intent to go through with the marriage.

One of the most important steps you can take to prepare for the legal stage of due diligence is to appoint good advisers. Don't scrimp on the calibre of your advisers, whether they're accountants, lawyers or tax consultants because good advisers in these areas will be worth their weight in gold as you move through the due diligence process, particularly when you reach the legal stage.

At this point the lawyers will be checking the parts of the business that may not have been checked during the viability assessment. It's another documentary, fact-checking stage essentially, but with a slightly different focus to what happens in the investigation stage. This is when lawyers will check the likes of intellectual property (IP) rights to make sure the IP is vested with the company and not owned by individuals, contractors or suppliers who are protected by copyright law.

IP can be a real risk for an investor, because they might think they're investing in a business that holds the IP to a particular product, only to discover it's held by an individual, contractor or supplier within that organisation. In the tech world, which is where we have a lot of experience, it's vital to thoroughly explore the IP of the technology owned by the business. Often IP issues won't come out until this final stage of due diligence, because this is when the lawyers will ask questions like:

- Who has been involved in developing the tech?
- Were they employees or contractors?
- What agreements are in place with these people?
- Is there an IP provision to ensure it's vested with the company?
- Are there registered trademarks or domains and are these owned by the company?
- Are there open-source (free-to-use software) licences in place?

The investors' legal team will also review your IT systems, disaster recovery plans, health and safety processes, employment terms and conditions and so on. Although you might have touched on some of this in the investigation stage, this is the point at which you dot the i's and cross the t's.

During the legal stage of due diligence, the investment documents and articles will be drafted. At this point you want to make sure you are in an open and honest scenario where all the cards are on the table, because when you enter into the final, binding contract you will be signing warranties in the agreements that state everything you have provided, given and told the investor was correct and complete at that point in time. In doing so, if something comes out of the woodwork later on then you can be liable for losses from investors if full disclosures weren't made, so it is vital that you are open and honest throughout the whole due diligence process.

If you think of this scenario in terms of getting married, it's as though you've walked down the aisle and said "I do", only to discover the following day that the person you've married was already married to someone else and that your marriage licence is now null and void. In business terms, this is the equivalent of failing to disclose aggressive tax planning that then leads to a large bill from HMRC. If your company is liable for that bill and your activities weren't disclosed to your investors during due diligence, they will want to be compensated because this information may well have affected their decision over whether to invest.

Summary

What we have provided here is an overview of the due diligence process, broken down into its three stages: evaluation, investigation and legal. In the coming chapters we're going to look in more detail at choosing the right funding options and preparing your pitch deck, which is the most important document for any investor.

Understanding what your funding options are and how to assess which are most appropriate for your business is essential and will have an impact on when you seek investment and who from. However, one of the most important elements to be clear on is how much investment you need and what you intend to use it for within your business and its broader growth plans. When it comes to becoming investable as a business, everything else follows on from knowing what your original funding request is and how realistic it is, which is where we'll start in Chapter 6.

Fast-growth insights

As we mentioned in Chapter 1, EHE invested in an insure-tech startup (Peppercorn) in 2022. The entrepreneur recognised how important the process was to secure investment, but found the process intense, and needed to do a lot of soul searching in the first two stages to ensure the proposition and concept could stand up to scrutiny. They admitted they underestimated the time and skills required for these steps and said, if they had their time again, they would bring in external support much sooner. The third stage was probably the toughest, as this was when the belief became a reality, but as advisors take their time to ensure an entrepreneur is aware of what they are signing, this stage also took longer than expected.

Whilst delays were inevitable, pushing through the last stage of the process was frustrating for the firm and entrepreneur in question. The key to enabling the investment to complet was ensuring all parties were kept up to date. One of the major lessons the entrepreneur learnt through this process was to never underestimate that final stage – this was when it got real.

CHAPTER SIX
FUNDING OPTIONS

As we've said, the starting point with seeking any form of funding for your business is to know how much you need and what you're going to need that money for. This should encompass not only what the money is going to be spent on, but also the results you expect to achieve or the value you expect to deliver by using that money for that specific purpose.

When you're searching for an investor, you want your relationship with them to be built on honesty, and that means being transparent about how much investment you require from the early stages of the process. We've all heard of people asking for, say, £2 million from their investors, only to come back a year later and ask for another £3 million. When you push them and ask why they didn't just ask for £5 million upfront, there are two common responses. The first is, "I knew I needed £5 million, but I didn't think I'd get that so I went in with £2 million because I thought that would be more likely." The second is, "I thought we could do this for £2 million but X, Y, Z has come up and that pushed us over budget."

In our experience, people often underestimate how much money they will need from an investor because they either have a tendency to think they can do certain things more cheaply than they really can, or because they think that if they go in looking for too large an amount of money that investors won't even look at their proposal. However, underestimating your funding needs ultimately doesn't help anyone. You have to be realistic about both what you're asking for and what you expect to achieve with the funding. You also need to build some slippage into your estimate of what you need, because this will give you a contingency to fall back on if things take longer or cost more than you anticipated.

The amount you ask for has to be well thought through. You can't simply ask for an arbitrary amount of money as an investment, because as soon as a potential investor digs into the figures behind your business they'll see that they don't add up, and that's going to make them wonder what it is you'll be spending their investment on. As we explained in the previous chapter, this process is a lot like entering into a relationship. That means both you and your investor want to go into this process with your eyes wide open.

We'll talk more about how to describe the opportunity you're offering investors in the next chapter when we talk about preparing your pitch deck. At this stage when we're looking purely at funding options, it's important to simply make sure you know exactly how much money you need and to be clear on what that money will be used for.

In addition to having this information clear in your mind, you also need to know what your business is valued at, how your business has been valued and how much equity in your company you're prepared to give away in exchange for the investment funds you need, which we'll discuss in more detail later in this chapter.

Without all of this information, an investor is not likely to step up and offer the funds that you need to help your business accelerate its growth. Bearing all of this in mind, let's explore the main funding options, and which ones are appropriate at which stage of your entrepreneurial journey.

Sweat equity

In very simple terms, sweat equity refers to your own time and money. If you are at the very beginning of your entrepreneurial journey, where you have an idea for a business and are still just dipping your toes in the water, you'll need to raise your own funding to get it off the ground. This might mean that you explore options such as remortgaging your house to access capital, or getting loans from family and friends. There are also some businesses for early stage founders who would be willing to provide services, or funds in exchange for equity. Borrowing money from family and friends in the early days of a business is one of the cheapest forms of finance because they are unlikely to expect big returns and this money will usually be loaned to you interest free.

Putting in your own money and taking on personal debt to get your business off the ground shows any future investors that you have skin in the game. You are invested in your business and you are committed to making it a success. This early stage can, naturally, be quite risky and the aim is to get the business to the next stage, where it becomes of interest to investors and other external funders.

EHE insight: *When you're taking investments from friends and family, it's better to treat them as loans. Offer to pay back the money with interest rather than giving them any equity in your business, otherwise as your business grows and you look at further investment, you'll be giving away more and more equity. The danger with giving away equity at this early stage is that you could end up with a number of people with a material shareholding in your business but who won't add any value on its journey beyond that initial small investment (rogue shareholders). The danger is having quite a big CAP table in your business early on, which significantly dilutes your shareholding as the founder. It's very important to hold onto as much of your shareholding in your business as you can in these early days, because this will give you more to play with when you go into later rounds of funding where you are looking for equity investors (more on this shortly).*

CAP Table

A table showing the ownership structure of your company. If you have a big CAP table, this means there are lots of different people involved in the ownership structure.

Debt funding

When you borrow money from banks or other debt providers, which usually has to be repaid with interest, this finance will be secured against an asset, usually one that's tangible, although there are some more inventive banks out there these days that will secure loans against intangible assets too. Bricks and mortar are the most traditional tangible assets against which debt providers secure loans. As an example of intangible assets, at the time of writing there are some debt providers that will finance a business based on its green credentials, whereby the business has to demonstrate that it's making a positive difference from an environmental point of view.

Banks can also provide debt funding based on concepts or designs, although this practice has been less prevalent since the first dot com bubble burst. It is possible to get funding on intellectual property (IP), provided it's inventive and ingenious in its construct.

All of that said, for entrepreneurial SMEs it is often quite hard to get debt funding, because the banks typically view businesses of this nature as quite high risk. A bank wants to see a consistent level of profit over a long period of time and the reality for most SMEs is that they haven't established that yet. In addition, most SMEs aren't looking to raise funds to buy bricks and mortar, which a bank could take security on, but to carry out activities that will grow the business. Even if those activities are part of a strategy and broader business plan, traditional banks consider this to be more uncertain because they always ask the question, "What if that doesn't happen? What's our security if things go wrong?"

As a result, banks will usually require personal guarantees from the people running and driving the business, which means you and the other directors of your business. Should things go wrong, you will therefore be on the hook individually for any debt you take on. This is one of the major downsides to debt funding in comparison to equity funding. Debt funding is not only risky for the business, because it has to pay that debt back, but also for the founders who will be on the hook personally if the business is unable to pay that debt back.

Invoice finance

Invoice finance is a specific type of debt, whereby you use your debtor book as an asset of your business to obtain funding. This will only work for established businesses, and this form of finance is typically quite expensive because the banks are taking on the risk that your customers (or debtors) may not pay. In general, businesses that sell products or services that customers take longer than 30 days to pay for are those best-suited to this form of finance.

If this is a route open to your company and one you would like to explore, you also need to consider taking out insurance to cover your business in the event that any of your customers don't pay their invoices. Again, this comes with a cost attached, so you need to factor this in when you are deciding whether invoice finance is a suitable route for your business to go down. Most companies that use this form of funding do so for working capital purposes, rather than to fund business growth.

Some debt funding providers will also factor in long-term contracts that your business has with clients, where they treat the amount you'll receive under the contract as being advanced to you now, knowing that it will come in even if not for a few years.

Equity funding

In essence, equity funding involves selling part of your company in exchange for a lump sum that you can use to support your growth and take your business to the next level.

Equity providers and debt providers differ fundamentally in their approach to the businesses they work with. Equity providers put their own skin in the game. The returns they get on the money they provide are entirely connected to the success of the business. As a result, equity providers will help you and work with you to ensure that your business succeeds.

Regardless of the type of business, if it fails it is the debt providers (banks) who are paid back first. They secure the money they provide against part of the business, knowing that either you will pay back your debt as agreed, or that they will be the first ones to be paid back should the business fail. Equity providers, on the other hand, take more risk because they won't receive any money if a business fails until all the debts have been paid off, and even then the amount they receive could well be lower than what they invested in the first place. Investors accept that, in the worst case scenario, they probably won't get anything back at all.

As equity providers take on greater risk than banks providing debt, they also expect higher returns on their investment.

The upside for you as an entrepreneur is that equity providers will be prepared to provide support and advice at any stage, because their success is tied to yours. You are both aligned to a common goal, which is generally a successful exit from the business.

In addition, the way in which your business is scrutinised when you seek equity funding as opposed to debt funding will be different. In Chapter 5 we talked about the due diligence process, which is when an investor will scrutinise a business to assess the structure, opportunity and risk. This process, of course, takes time and there is often a lot of back and forth between you (and your team) and the potential investor (and their team). This allows you to finesse your ask and negotiate over what you need and the best way to achieve your goals. You will also receive advice from the potential investor about the best way to move forward with your business growth plans.

When you apply for debt funding you and your business will still be assessed, although the process is somewhat different. While the application itself for this type of funding may be simpler, your business will still be scrutinised and this process may not be a great deal quicker than that for equity funding. One of the big differences is that once you submit an application for debt funding, you won't have the opportunity to change your figures or what you're asking for. Once you set this process in motion it has to play out and go through all the steps, with a yes or no answer coming at the end, and no advice along the way.

Different levels of equity investors

There are three main levels of equity funding and investors. Each will be applicable at a different stage of your business' growth and they all take different approaches to investing.

Angel investors: Angel investors tend to select businesses to work with based more on gut feel than a huge amount of information. They often come into a business at an early stage when the risk is greatest, such as in the startup or proof of concept phase. While they will provide funds to support you in the early stages of your business, they also take a fair proportion of your equity in exchange. Angel investors tend to be private high-net-worth individuals and usually they invest between £50,000 and £100,000.

First-round investors: At this stage, your business will be considered a medium risk. You'll have built up your revenue and you'll have proved your concept but you need an influx of funding to help you take your business to the next level (this is typically where we as the EHE Group find our sweet spot). You'll have all the right ingredients in place to achieve fast growth, but you need additional funding and potentially advice to help you get there. Investors at this stage are usually private individuals and can offer more than angel investors, generally their investments are in the low hundreds of thousands.

Second – and third-round investors: Second and third-round investors are very similar, and generally fall under the private equity and venture capital umbrellas. They are very different investors to those who you will work with at the angel and first-round stages. You need the help of private equity investors when your business is experiencing stratospheric growth and you simply need more capital to keep momentum going. Because private equity firms have access to a much larger pot of money, they will be able to provide funding in the millions, rather than the hundreds of thousands.

At each stage, the amount of equity you give away in your business will get progressively lower, because the risk diminishes as the business grows and becomes more stable. When you get to the second – and third-round investment, debt financing may become more attractive because you want to keep hold of as much equity as possible, whereas each time you raise funds via equity investors, you dilute the equity in the business.

Balancing your need with the business' valuation

It's important to consider what percentage of your company's equity you are prepared to give away when you seek investment, but be careful when you work this out that you are not basing your decision solely on your business' value today. Remember that the whole point of the investment you're seeking is to grow your business

For example, imagine your business is worth £1 million and you are only prepared to give away a 20 per cent equity stake, which equates to £200,000 of its current value. However, to achieve the growth you're aiming for, you actually need £400,000, and to receive that level of investment you will need to give up more than 20 per cent of the equity. This links back into mindset, because when you take a step back you can see that having a smaller stake in a business that is considerably larger will actually mean you have more than keeping a higher stake in a much smaller business.

It can help to think of it like this: would you rather have an 80 per cent stake in a business that's worth £2 million, or a 60 per cent stake in a business that's worth £10 million? While you have to be careful about giving away equity too early on in the process, you also need to be mindful of how much you can achieve if you're prepared to give away a bit more equity to the right funding partner.

Depending on what stage your business is at, you also need to consider future opportunities for offering equity to investors. Let's imagine your business is valued at £1 million and you give an angel investor a 20 per cent stake for £200,000. Around 18 months to two years later, you might need a second round of funding. At this stage, you might offer another investor a further 20 per cent equity stake, but because of what you've achieved as a result of that initial £200,000 investment, now a 20 per cent stake in your company is worth £2 million. Of course, as the founder you're diluting your stake in the business each time you do this, but you're still considerably better off than you would have been had you held onto 100 per cent of your company and not received any external funding.

A note on provisions for buying shares back
In Chapter 3, we introduced the concept of rogue shareholders, and why it's important to be mindful about who you offer shares to, especially during the early stages of your business. If you are giving shares in the business to employees or even early investors, it's important to have what are known as good and bad leaver provisions in place to allow you to acquire back the shareholdings when someone is no longer involved with the business.

A bad leaver provision allows shares to be acquired back for par value, which is quite often a pound. A good leaver provision, meanwhile, allows shares to be acquired back for their current market value. Often this provision would be enacted when an employee retires, or leaves the business due to ill health, for example. In addition to these relatively simple mechanisms for buying back shares, there may also be terms that allow an employee to vest a certain percentage of their shares. For example, if someone works for your company for three years and then leaves, allowing them to vest a percentage of their shares acknowledges the value they brought to the business in that time. In this example, if the employee had a two per cent share option, after three years they may have vested 50 per cent of those shares and therefore when they leave they are allowed to keep one per cent of their shares. This is really important to consider if you will be seeking investment in the future, because without shareholder agreements and mechanisms to recover shares where necessary, you are likely to be viewed as uninvestable.

What support will you get?

It's also important to consider what level of support you will get with each different funding option. This is particularly crucial if you are in the early stages of your business or on the cusp of fast growth, because being able to tap into the expertise and experience of investors who have built and sold their own companies can be invaluable to accelerate your company's growth.

Many startups and businesses in their early stages simply can't afford people with a high level of experience in everything from sales and marketing to finance and operations. However, with the right investor you can get access to such skills without having to outlay significant amounts. We always want to support the entrepreneurs we work with and challenge them to find the most efficient ways to grow their businesses, without getting directly involved in the operational side of things.

When you're seeking equity financing, you are bringing partners into your business in the form of your investors. You therefore want to ensure that your investors are a good fit and aligned, not only personally, but also behind the same goals and values for the business. As an entrepreneur, this means you have to think about more than just the cash you'll be receiving from your investors and also consider the expertise they'll be bringing to your business. This is all about how an equity investor can support you during the business' growth and, clearly, if you are well aligned it makes working together towards that common goal much easier.

In the last chapter we talked about the due diligence process, and what an investor looks for in a business and entrepreneur before they commit to providing equity funding. However, it is just as important for you to carry out your own due diligence on any potential providers of equity funding, to ensure they are a good fit for your business and that you are aligned on the key areas of focus for the business.

Finding the right investor and financing option

There is a lot to consider when you're seeking investment for your business, and choosing the right financing option, as well as the right investor, is crucial. For many entrepreneurs, seeking secured finance via a bank will be a waste of time and energy, because the chances of being refused are quite high, while you also won't receive any additional advice or support alongside the cash even if you are approved for a loan.

At EHE Group, we not only provide advice and guidance to entrepreneurs who are seeking equity funding, but we also assess the business need and, if debt financing would be more appropriate, we will recommend that you speak to a bank rather than going through the process of seeking an equity investor. If, however, equity finance is the right option for you and your business, we'll then work with you to structure the opportunity from both a business and strategic perspective to help you position it in the right way when you get in front of investors.

Whatever stage your business is at, and regardless of what route you believe you should go down to finance its growth, it's important to seek professional advice. Your accountant and/or financial director are a good first port of call. They will be able to outline the pros and cons of debt finance and equity investment, which is a good place to begin before you take any further steps.

EHE insight: When you are looking for an equity investor, be mindful of any upfront fees you may get asked to pay by organisations that are assisting with your search for an investor. Where possible, you want to avoid being tied into upfront fees and other charges, because this adds an unnecessary debt burden to the business. Instead, it is beneficial to find an organisation that will attach any such fees to the end of the process, once you have been able to realise the fast growth you want to use the investment for.

Summary

This chapter is designed to give you an overview of the main funding options available and to outline the pros and cons of each. Of course, every business will be different and therefore there is no one-size-fits-all approach to finding investment. Having all the foundations we've discussed so far in place will, however, make your journey to investment smoother, whatever form that investment comes in.

One of the key things to remember when it comes to choosing between equity finance or debt finance is that when you receive equity finance you are getting far more than just the money. The advice and experience of the right investor can prove invaluable and set your company on a fast-growth trajectory. Finding the right investor can be a challenge in itself, which is why putting together a strong pitch deck is so important.

Fast-growth insights

You don't know what you don't know; most entrepreneurs assume they want to raise money through equity investment because that's what they read about in the media. This isn't always the right way, however.

An entrepreneur we were advising assumed he needed to raise money through equity investment. However, as we got into the details we realised he could fund his business in stages via bank debt and sales cash flow without the need for any equity funding. The result was he kept 100 per cent equity in his company.

Another example is in the aviation industry where the entrepreneurs in a three-phased growth and development plan thought they needed to raise money at the risky (expensive equity) R&D stage. In actual fact, they didn't and ended up funding it themselves with a government grant with no loss of equity.

Part 3: The Business –
Getting Investor Ready

CHAPTER SEVEN
PREPARING
YOUR PITCH DECK

In Chapter 5 we explored how to prepare for due diligence and one of the most important documents to prepare is your pitch deck. We can't stress enough how crucial it is for helping you get through that initial evaluation stage of due diligence. This is where you get to tell your story. As investors, we're looking for something that's brief and simple, but that captures our imaginations too.

The purpose of your pitch deck

The purpose of your pitch deck is to get investors excited about your company so that they want to progress to the second stage of due diligence. Your story is a fundamental part of this, so it's worth taking the time to make sure it's told in an engaging, entertaining and simple way. Your pitch deck should not be too long. You will have a window of no more than 20 minutes, but the first five minutes need to be impactful to capture the heart and mind of the investor. This is how long they'll look at your pitch deck before making a decision about whether to proceed. Use it wisely.

Of course, your pitch deck is about more than just your story as an entrepreneur. It needs to very clearly state why you need investment and how much investment you're asking for. Making this obvious and putting it up front is key. You also need to clearly demonstrate what you're offering in return for that investment.

Your pitch deck also needs to identify any problems you're facing and outline how you will approach the solutions. Keep this realistic and make sure that any figures you provide are accurate, as these will be investigated at the next stage of due diligence.

EHE insight: Pictures, illustrations and diagrams often speak louder than words. Use these at the front of your pitch deck if you can and provide further details in the appendices of your pitch deck should the investor want more detail.

It's also essential to answer the question of "Why you, and not somebody else?", particularly if you are operating in a saturated market. The investors you're approaching might also be looking at other companies in the same industry, so you need to be able to articulate why you are different to your competitors, what your USP is and why you are the better investment opportunity. Think about any objections an investor might have and tackle those in your pitch deck when you can.

Finding the balance in your pitch deck

Putting together a strong pitch deck is a real art and you have to strike the right balance between providing a succinct and exciting overview of your company and its story and why it's a great opportunity for investors, with figures and details that demonstrate your company is on the path to fast growth and will be a good investment.

We recommend having no more than 10 to 15 slides in your pitch deck and then using appendices where you can provide more detail for those who are interested in reading it. It can help to think of your pitch deck as a synopsis of your business plan. Your full business plan will be examined in detail once you reach the second stage of due diligence: investigation. Of course, depending on the stage your business is at, a pitch deck and a business plan can be the same thing. This would likely be the case for a startup seeking investment, for example.

However, if your business has been established for a number of years and has evolved, your business plan and your pitch deck shouldn't be the same, because you will have a lot more data and detail that you can include in a business plan from your initial years of operation.

It can also help to think of your pitch deck as a showreel for your company; this is where you get to show off the highlights and present you and your business in the best possible light. This is the tip of the iceberg, but you want to demonstrate that there is more under the surface that is providing solid support for the tip of your iceberg.

Pitch deck principles

Use the following as a guide of what to include when you're putting together your pitch deck. Not all businesses need all of these sections, so take what you need to effectively showcase your business to potential investors.

- **Executive summary and proposition:** This needs to explain who you are, what you want and why. Keep it brief (one page) and include a brief history of the company, a brief overview of the opportunity (your unique selling point), what you are asking for and what you are offering. This slide needs to be powerful because it's your opening gambit.

- **The problem:** Clearly state the problem your service/product solves and explain why the current solution is broken or non-existent. Don't forget to cover current industry issues if they're relevant too.

- **The solution:** Explain your approach to the problem and why it's effective. If your solution is unique, explain why.

- **Target market and opportunity:** Cover your route to market, what/who you're targeting, the size of the market and your target share. Mention any barriers to entry and/or regulatory obligations and explain how you're tackling them. An overview of the competitive landscape is also useful.

- **Competition and competitive advantage:** Explain how you will compete with your competitors, why you're better, what your key advantage is and what's stopping them copying your approach.

- **Team:** Provide an overview of your operating structure, what your hiring plan is and how you're structuring your business to take advantage of the opportunity you outlined at the start of your pitch.

- **Key milestones:** Provide a graphical representation of your company's formation, previous investments, first-round funding, key hires, first profit, geographical expansion plans and further funding (if applicable).

- **Revenue or business model:** Be very clear about how your business makes money and break it down if it's complex! Cover your high-level business plan, including cashflow management and timings, as well as highlighting growth opportunities. These include key revenue streams and any supporting information on potential returns. If you have one, a more in-depth investment management plan would also fit here.

- **Marketing and sales strategy:** Share your top-level marketing plan and be clear about what you plan to spend your investment on. Include data points such as cost per acquisition and how much you're spending on your marketing and sales strategy. Explain how this will ramp up in line with the business and revenue model and highlight any spikes in marketing spend (customer acquisition via loss leaders and offers etc.).

- **Financials:** Give a financial overview, sharing your trading performance to date. Explain how you will fund fast growth. Talk about the investment and how you'll use those funds.
- **Contact details:** Make sure your website and social media, as well as your email and phone number, are on this slide.
- **Appendix:** The place for any supporting information, data sources, case studies, reviews etc.

Who should write the pitch deck?

As the entrepreneur behind the business you have to take ownership of creating the pitch deck because it is telling (and selling) your story. No one will ever be able to tell your story better than you can, and if you don't feel that you can tell your story then you have to ask how you're going to get anyone else to believe in it or understand it. Let your passion for what you do come through in the slides.

That said, often as an entrepreneur you might have a great idea and a good overall understanding of your business, but you may lack specific expertise in some areas. This is when it's important to work with the experts within your business to make sure you are filling in any gaps in your knowledge and providing investors with the answers to the questions they are most likely to ask.

Remember that investors like to invest in people and their ideas, not in slides, so talk about the team you have behind you. You might have a great product, but an investor is going to want to know how you're going to produce it and bring it to market, and that will come from the team you have in place (or are putting in place). This is why we have a whole chapter earlier in the book about selecting the right management team!

Play to your strengths

Like many people, you might be picturing the TV show Dragon's Den when you think of delivering a pitch for investment. Presenting your pitch deck verbally is one option, but it's not essential when you're seeking investment. Whether you want to take this approach will depend on both you and the investor you are pitching to.

If you will be delivering your pitch deck to investors in-person, think carefully about who you want to bring into the room with you. If you know that you're great at talking about your story and that your passion really shines through, but that you struggle to remember the finer details about operations and finance, make sure you have at least one member of your management team with you who can provide that important supporting information.

If you know you come across better when you're speaking than you will in slides, another option is to record a two – to three-minute video that you can include in your first slide. This can then be followed up with the detail that an investor will look for next in written slides. This can be especially effective for investors who have a shorter attention span and need to be drawn in within the first minute or two of looking at a pitch.

Should you tailor your pitch deck?

Deciding whether or not to tailor your pitch deck can be tricky. Much like when you're applying for a job, in an ideal world you would tailor your CV to suit each role and business. However, when you're sending dozens of job applications a month this simply isn't practical (or necessarily a good use of your time). It's very similar when it comes to tailoring your pitch deck.

In some cases you may decide it is worth taking the extra time to tailor your pitch deck. For example, if you have researched a particular investor and believe they will be a great fit for your business, you may decide to tailor some of the slides to appeal to this specific investor. However, the reality is that you will likely need to go through multiple rounds of pitching with different investors, which means tailoring your pitch deck every time won't be practical.

In general, your pitch deck needs to cater for all investors. What you want to avoid is turning some investors off by leaning too heavily in a particular direction. For instance, as we write this book there is an increased focus on diversity and inclusion (D&I) and environmental, social and corporate governance (ESG). Some investors are certainly making decisions based purely on these elements; however, if you tailor your pitch deck too heavily towards a D&I or ESG audience, you risk alienating investors who might be catching up in these areas, but who aren't quite there yet. That said, these are not areas that are nice to have. Investors will expect to see some content around D&I and ESG, so make sure this is included in your pitch deck.

Of course, if D&I or ESG (or both) is particularly relevant to you and your business, it is certainly worth highlighting that side of your business, because in doing so you are more likely to connect with and therefore attract investors who also value these things. If, as an entrepreneur, you clearly align with and focus on these areas, you may find there are some funding options that are particularly applicable to you, such as investors looking for female-led businesses, or those led by people from ethnic minorities. The key, as with everything, is balance so that you're not pigeonholing yourself unnecessarily.

How to help your pitch deck stand out

Investors will more than likely see dozens of pitch decks each week, so it's important to think about how you can make yours stand out from the crowd for all the right reasons. This is where your PR and personal branding can make a real difference.

In this day and age, most investors are active on social media channels (especially LinkedIn) and consume local news (or industry-specific news depending on their focus). This means that if they have already seen you and your business either featuring in news outlets or on their LinkedIn feed, your pitch deck is more likely to jump out to them simply because you are known to them.

This goes beyond what's included in the pitch deck itself, because it's about what approach you're taking to promoting yourself and your business in general. Putting this groundwork in not only benefits your business, but also means that you are more likely to get noticed by investors when you do come to send pitch decks in.

Common pitfalls to avoid

There are some simple mistakes entrepreneurs can make when creating and sending pitch decks that are very easily avoided.

1. *Using pitch deck templates*

It can be very easy to search online for a pitch deck template; you will find dozens of examples within seconds. However, be very cautious about using these. We have seen pitch decks in the past where it is very obvious the person in question has taken an existing pitch deck from another business and simply overlaid their information on it. We have even seen examples where the other company's name has been left in a footer on the page!

This is a very easily avoidable situation. When an investor sees this in a pitch deck, they question your passion. It will make your whole pitch deck feel impersonal, because they can clearly see you've just filled in boxes rather than tailoring your pitch deck to really show off your business in its best light.

2. *Failing to check the figures*

Whatever concrete data or financial information you're sharing in your pitch deck, you have to make sure it adds up. We have seen pitch decks where the income less the costs to the business doesn't equate to the figure that the business is presenting as its profit. This is very easy to spot (and should therefore also be easy to correct when you are putting your pitch deck together).

When we see this as investors, we immediately start to question what else might not add up, or what else might have been missed. It breaks trust before it has even been built.

3. *Including too much information*

You have to find the right balance between providing enough information for investors to see that you have a strong business and providing so much information that investors feel overwhelmed. We have seen pitch decks of 40 or more slides and it's just overkill. An investor doesn't want to wade through that much detail at this stage in the process, they simply want the salient points and top-level figures.

4. *Using too much jargon or too many acronyms*

You have to get your language right and avoid using too many technical terms and jargon in your pitch deck. Keep it simple and keep it to the point. Make sure that it's easy to understand and, where jargon is unavoidable, make sure it's clearly explained. Avoid acronyms unless they're essential and always make sure they are spelled out. Don't assume that the person reading your pitch deck will know what an acronym stands for.

5. *Including too much text*

When it comes to pitch decks, less is generally more. Don't try to fill each slide with text. Use bullet points rather than writing lengthy paragraphs. Use graphs and other diagrams to display information in a way that's easy to visualise and understand. Don't be tempted to reduce the font size to fit more in (we can remember one pitch deck that used font size four!), it doesn't help. All this does is demonstrate that you have no concept of how to keep your business simple.

6. *Spelling and grammatical mistakes*

Make sure you proofread your pitch deck before you send it out. If you know this isn't your strength, find someone who has a good eye for spelling and grammar to look over it for you. Sending out a pitch deck littered with spelling and grammatical errors shows a lack of care and attention.

7. *Failing to talk enough about you*

While it's important to address your position in the marketplace and cover the business landscape and your main competitors, you have to remember that the pitch deck is fundamentally about you and your business. If you spend 80 per cent of it critiquing other businesses without telling the investors why you're unique and how you will improve on what's already out there, your pitch deck will fall flat.

8. *Misrepresenting yourself*

Your pitch deck has to be an accurate reflection of you, because this is what the investor is buying into. Investors want to find entrepreneurs who align with them and who are a good fit. Obviously if you're pretending to be someone you're not in your pitch deck, you'll run into conflict somewhere along the line. Make sure you're honest and true to yourself and that you allow your passion to shine through. Don't tell people what you think they want to hear, tell people about you and your business. Remember that what an investor really wants to hear is your story.

9. *Know who you're sending your pitch decks to*

It might sound basic, but make sure that you have the right email addresses for the investors you're approaching. Check the spelling of their name and address the email personally to them. If you are going to personalise your pitch deck, make sure you do your research so that you hit the right mark. These kinds of mistakes are easy to make and very hard (if not impossible) to recover from.

Keep it simple

Remember that your pitch deck is an overview of your business that's designed to whet the appetite of an investor, it doesn't need to be lengthy. We recommend 10 to 15 slides, because this is enough to give you space to cover the key points and information an investor will expect to and want to see, without going overboard on the details. That said, if you can distil all the essential information into five slides, don't feel as though you need to stretch your pitch deck to 10 slides. The pitch deck principles we shared earlier in this chapter are there to act as a guide, but if not everything we've listed there is relevant to your business, don't shoe-horn it in.

The information most investors will want to see is:

- Have you thought about your problem?
- Have you got the right approach to the solution?
- What is the marketing opportunity?
- Who is part of your team?
- What is your revenue model to reach your market?
- What is your marketing and sales strategy?

Try to capture all of this as simply as you can in as few slides as possible. Think about how you can best present certain data. For example, we recently saw a pitch deck where the entrepreneur had used a diagram to highlight the USP they were driving for, which in this case was cost and route to market. By making it visual, they presented a really powerful comparison of their business compared to the major players in their market. It was one slide that created the "wow" factor. By slide four, we were sold. Had that entrepreneur explained this in writing, it would likely have covered two or more slides and would not have had the same impact.

As well as the information you're putting in your pitch deck, think about how it's structured. Make sure you cover your key points in a logical order for the investor and don't use 20 words where five will do. Visual elements can be incredibly useful for showcasing complex information so think about how you can incorporate these into your pitch deck.

Summary

Your pitch deck is a vital part of the process for raising funding for your business. You have to get this right if you want to progress through due diligence and get to the investigation and then the legal stages. If you don't, you'll fall at the first hurdle. Your pitch deck needs to create enough intrigue in the investor that they want to pick up the phone and have a conversation with you without drowning them in information. It needs to demonstrate your passion, because ultimately this is what the investor will be investing in.

However, it's important that whatever you include in your pitch deck can be substantiated with detailed information, because this is what any investor will be looking for when they decide to move into the next stage of the process.

Your pitch deck is the gateway to investment conversations. It is one of the first hurdles you need to overcome on the road to investment to grow your business. If you think of it like applying for a job, this is the equivalent of submitting your CV. If you don't send your CV out, you won't even be considered for a job. If you don't send your pitch deck out, you won't be considered for investment.

Only if your CV is appealing do you get invited for an interview (the investigation stage of due diligence) and from there move into negotiation. It's no different when it comes to seeking investment. Sending your pitch deck is the first active step you'll take towards seeking investment, even if you have been building strong foundations for your business for a while, as we talked about earlier in the book.

Now that you understand what's required to get an investor's interest, what funding options are available to you and what due diligence entails, we're going to cover one more important element that you need to consider: your exit strategy.

Fast-growth insights

We've said several times that investors invest in people, and this is why personal branding and PR is so vital. One of the first investments Gary and Ross were involved in together hinged on exactly this. The business in question was trying to secure a lot of investment at a time when the business made no money at all. There were assets for security, but the investors' decision to support the entrepreneurs was based on their confidence in them to deliver their growth aspirations.

Gary and Ross looked at the entrepreneurs' social profiles, what they had done and how they had integrated into the business community to inform their decision. Ultimately, the question was: could they trust these people to deliver fast growth? Based on what they knew of them, they believed they could.

That pitch might well have gone very differently had the entrepreneurs in question not had that presence in their business community and online. It all comes back to being able to show investors why they should choose you and not somebody else.

PART 4:
FAST
FORWARD...

In this final part of the book, we look at preparing to exit your business and what steps you can take to maximise shareholder value, as well as what the future of investing holds.

There is a great deal of crossover in what we have discussed in Part 3 around becoming investor ready and preparing to exit your business. Essentially, if you take the steps we recommend to make your business attractive to investors, you are getting ahead of the curve when it comes to preparing to exit and maximising shareholder value.

While preparing the business for your exit is essential, so too is preparing yourself emotionally for the process of leaving a business that you have likely spent years, if not decades, working on.

In the penultimate chapter, we'll look at the three core areas that investors are focusing on, namely tech and tech-led businesses, environmental credentials and strong social responsibility practices. This means focusing on any (or all) of these areas within your organisation can help your business to be more attractive to both investors and acquirers.

In Chapter 10, we'll explore what recessions mean for fast-growth businesses and explain why they are not as negative as the media makes them appear. In fact, when you focus on looking for opportunities rather than worrying about the state of the economy, a recession presents a chance for your business to thrive.

Part 4: Fast Forward…

CHAPTER EIGHT
THE EXIT

When it comes to being exit ready there are two elements to consider: yourself as the entrepreneur and the business. We'll start by looking at what you need to do to be ready to exit the business as an entrepreneur, and then we'll talk about the business itself.

Are you ready to exit?

Your mindset is one of the most crucial factors when it comes to being exit ready on an individual level. We talked at length about the mindset you need to achieve fast growth in Chapter 2, but the mindset you need to successfully exit your business is slightly different. When you are considering exiting your business, the question you have to ask yourself is, "Are you ready to get out?" In many cases, you will have spent years, quite possibly decades, building up a business and it can be challenging to reach a point at which you are comfortable walking away from that and leaving it in someone else's hands, no matter how capable they are.

What you will often find is that, at some point in your entrepreneurial journey, you start to think about an exit from your business. This isn't the kind of decision that tends to be made overnight. This is your starting point for getting your mindset in the right place to actually exit your business, even if that's years in the future.

Chipping

Chipping is a common strategy used by acquirers. Essentially they make you an offer with a headline figure and then towards the end of the process, usually as you're finishing due diligence, they 'chip' you on the price. They do this on the basis that the entrepreneur has already spent the money in their head and that they're getting excited about receiving what will likely be the largest cheque they've ever had.

As an entrepreneur, you're getting on an emotional rollercoaster when you accept an offer, but it doesn't end here. You then have to go through the due diligence process, which can be stressful if you're being warned to expect a 'chip' at any time. "I thought I was handling that stage well," Guy reveals, "But after the deal had gone through one or two of the other execs told me they could see I was becoming more emotional the closer we got to finalising the sale."

It's important to be prepared for this emotional journey, because it will take a little while for the amount you're being paid for your business to truly sink in. It will be a life-changing sum of money and it's when you start to think about what that will mean for you, your family and your other executives that you start to become more emotional. Typically this will happen at some point during due diligence, which means you'll start to worry about what they might find, even if you know you have a very solid and well-run company.

You also have to prepare yourself emotionally for the possibility that the deal may fall through, even at a late stage. There is so much that can go wrong that is completely out of your control, from recessions and wars to global pandemics. All you can do is focus on the process and resist the urge to start spending the money before it has landed in your bank account.

Once you get through the due diligence stage, you then have the period where you're handing over to the new management, which, as we'll explain a little later in this chapter, can sometimes drag out – especially if you are then in the mindset of wanting to exit your business.

How to get acquired

It's always far better if you allow potential acquirers to approach you, rather than going out in search of someone to buy your business. When your business is good enough to sell, people will have heard about you and this will mean they are more likely to approach you.

If you're approached, this puts you on the front foot. And if your natural reaction to an approach is, "No, I'm not selling," then you're really on the front foot because you will discover how badly the person looking to buy really wants you. In terms of tactics, it is generally beneficial to play slightly hard to get if you can. However, it's like any business decision and you will have to make an educated guess as to the best way to approach it and play it the best way you can.

One thing you definitely don't want to do, however, is look desperate, because the second you look desperate you won't get the value out of the business that you deserve.

That said, it's not uncommon for businesses to let it be known that they are on the market. You don't have to do this overtly, but you can let a couple of agents know and word will get around. You might even drop the odd hint here or there in conversations you're having in your business networks and you'll be surprised at how quickly word spreads when you do.

Very often, trade sales are the best ones to make when you're selling your business, because you're more likely to get better money for your business and there's a better chance it will be acquired by a more appropriate organisation to take it forward. Of course that's not guaranteed, but in most industries there will be very good trade buyers out there.

The difference when you are acquired by a private equity firm is that the focus is very much on the figures and that firm will be thinking about how it is going to exit from the business in a few short years, often by selling to another private equity company. As an entrepreneur, you can still have a very profitable acquisition through a private equity firm, if you play your cards right. Our preference, however, would usually be for a trade sale (when we have a choice) because these companies are usually buying you for a specific reason, whether that's your team or because they want to develop the business.

What's your number?

When it comes to exiting your business, the price you are offered will obviously play a role. Every entrepreneur has a number in their head for the value of their business; sometimes it's logical and sometimes it's not. That doesn't really matter, because if someone matches that number or offers above it, you will likely accept that offer.

However, (and this is where the logic comes in) it's important to understand that every sector has a multiple and this is what's used to calculate the value of a business. For example, the multiple in your sector might be eight times your EBITDA, or it might be four times, or even 12 times that value. This means when a buyer comes knocking, they will generally have applied that multiple to your business to help them come up with a value for it. The reason trade buyers often offer higher prices than private equity is that they will be able to absorb your business into theirs and make efficiencies, thereby enabling them to make a higher multiple.

It's also important to acknowledge that the market can play a role in the valuation your company receives. All markets move in cycles and we all know that this means some industries will be in favour while others will be out. In some cases this can circle back around, but it is worth bearing in mind whether this means your business is particularly relevant at a certain time. Guy's experience with Cake is a good example of this, because the technology they used was very relevant when the offer came in, so the timing for an exit was ideal. You can't underestimate timing.

We have also seen entrepreneurs be too greedy and turn down good offers that have been on the table because they have an unrealistic number in their head. Then the market or the business has gone against them and they've gone downhill and not been able to achieve a similarly good offer in the future.

This is when having a good board and good advisers is incredibly valuable. It is very useful to have people around you who will check you and point out that what you've got is a good offer at the right time. These people, especially any non-execs who have been through this process themselves, will help lift you out of the emotion of the situation and talk to you about it logically.

It's only natural to feel emotional about selling a business that you've been involved with for ten, 15 or more years. You've been on a journey with that company, but you do need those people around you who can be a bit more logical and help you take an objective look at what is being offered.

Preparing your company for an exit

We mentioned the practice of chipping during an acquisition and while this does happen quite often, it's not a given. For example, when Guy sold Cake, there was no chip in the offer. One of the most important things you can do to prevent a chip from coming when you are selling your business is to ensure that it's well run.

This comes back to everything we've talked about in previous chapters in relation to getting your business investor ready. You need the right team around you, from senior managers to experienced non-execs. You need your operations to be run professionally to ensure they stand up to the scrutiny of due diligence. In fact, the due diligence process is very similar whether you are looking for investment or exiting your business, so if you prepare well for due diligence ahead of seeking investment you will be in a strong position for any acquisition offers that come your way too.

The point is that in getting your ducks in a row in this way, you are reducing risk within the business and you are not giving potential acquirers any reasons to chip your offer down. It's therefore very prudent to take these steps a few years before you're thinking about exiting, because if you don't you could literally lose millions.

It's also important to remember that, if or when that chip does come, you have a choice; you don't have to sell. Whether or not you make that decision will more than likely depend on how legitimate that chip is. Has the acquirer genuinely discovered something during due diligence that gives them cause to believe there's more risk, or is it spurious to reduce the price?

If you do have everything in your business in order, it will really strengthen your hand when you come to exit. Gary recollects that when he sold his business, the buyer paid an external organisation to phone 1,000 of their customers to find out what they thought of them. "It was a magical moment actually, because they couldn't find one out of that 1,000 who didn't love us! Our net promoter score was higher than Apple, which is pretty mind blowing, and this just reinforced how strong we were on customer service and therefore reinforced the price of the business," he says.

Much of what you have to do to prepare your business for your exit is the same as what we've discussed throughout this book in terms of preparing for fast growth and investment. However, the biggest difference when you're preparing for an acquisition is that you have to demonstrate that you have achieved fast growth, and that the business can continue to grow, with or without you (the entrepreneur) at the helm. This is different from when you're seeking an initial investment and you only have to demonstrate that your business has good *potential* and the *capabilities* to achieve fast growth.

Creating a Self-Managing Company®

Ultimately what you're aiming to do ahead of seeking an acquisition is create a self-managing company that no longer relies on you, the entrepreneur, to function. You want everything to be running so smoothly that you could leave for six months and your business would continue to thrive. If you can reach this stage with your business, your exit will be a lot less painful – for you, your team, the business and the acquirer.

When your company is self-managing and no longer relies on you, this will come through in the due diligence. Your team will acknowledge that you are the one who sprinkles a bit of fairy dust every now and then, but it will also be apparent that everything can operate without you and this puts you in a much stronger position to exit and be acquired.

Carefully managing risk when seeking investment

Although this chapter is about being exit ready, it's important that you begin to think about the possibility of exiting your business before you seek investment, because this will mean you are more effective at managing the associated risks. An important part of this process is ensuring you have the support of a strong legal team, because you will need them to go over the details associated with any investment.

Our first piece of advice is not to wait until you receive the legal agreement to discuss shareholding agreements when you're seeking investment. The reason is simply that the legal agreement typically arrives very late in the process. Often investors will want to use what are known as preference or alphabet shares. Simply this means that some shareholders will get preference over others when it comes to receiving payouts. If you discover this in the legal agreement, it might be too late to do much about it.

Instead we recommend having all of these discussions when you are agreeing the term sheet or heads of terms during due diligence. You have to bear in mind that an investor will have done this many times before and therefore will know about all the pitfalls and where to slide things in late in the day. If you're not aware of these potential pitfalls at this stage, it can come back to bite you when you are looking to exit your business.

One key term to remember (and use where possible in relation to shares) is "pari passu". This means your shares as the entrepreneur are treated exactly the same as the investor's shares. This will become particularly pertinent when you get to the "distribution waterfall".

Pari passu

A means of ensuring that your interests and the investor's interests are treated equally. This doesn't only apply to shares and can also apply to dividends and exit payments.

The distribution waterfall simply refers to who gets paid first. Generally the bank will be paid first (if your business carries any debt), followed by the mezzanine finance provider (if there is one). If your investor has preference shares, they will come next. Finally, at the bottom of the list will be you and your management team. You might think that sounds ok, but let's just explore an example of how much (or how little) that could leave you with.

This all comes back to the risk a company carries. Most investors will get as much debt into the business as possible. Let's therefore say the bank has a 70 per cent stake. On top of this, you take out mezzanine finance, which is a bit riskier, and that covers a 15 per cent stake. This means your company is now 85 per cent leveraged and that presents a risk. If your investor has a coupon of 10 per cent per annum of their investment, that has to come out of the business next. If that investor has put £40 million in, that's a £4 million payment each year. The question then is what's left for you, the entrepreneur?

If you're in a situation like this, your company will need to perform pretty well to leave you with anything. Obviously you will work as hard as you need to in order to achieve growth, but there is a risk here; namely that if there's nothing left after all those other payments have been made, you're left with nothing. When this happens, we describe a business and entrepreneur as being "underwater".

However, if you make sure you are "pari passu" with your investor, you have a greater chance of being paid out at the end. It means you're sharing that risk with your investor, rather than the investor getting off mildly and you and your management team taking a big hit if things don't go to plan.

We don't mean to scare you with these details, but it's important that you're well informed about how different shareholder agreements work. There might be a situation when you're prepared to compromise and agree to a particular investor having preference shares because you want to work with them, but at least that is an informed choice on your part and not a nasty surprise.

Understanding the next steps in an acquisition

Once the acquisition has been agreed and you've gone through the due diligence process, there will be a few more steps to clear before you officially exit your business. One of the first to be aware of is warranties, which you and your management team have to agree to warrant that what you've shared about the business is correct and that you haven't left anything out. There will be financial penalties if the acquirer discovers you have lied or left something material out of your disclosures.

It is also common to leave some money in the business, usually in escrow, in case there are financial penalties you have to pay. This is often used in relation to property purchases, but it is also used for business acquisitions.

Escrow

A legal agreement whereby a third party holds a large sum of money until a particular condition or conditions have been met.

The amount you have to leave in escrow will be dictated by how much your business is being acquired for. The argument from the acquirer will usually be that, unless you have something to hide, you shouldn't mind leaving a couple of million in escrow for an agreed amount of time, normally one to two years.

The criteria you have to meet to clear escrow will also vary from business to business. For example, when Guy sold Cake, their criteria related to the number of people who left the business in the first 18 months after the acquisition, because the company had primarily been bought because of the team and their expertise. Once the 18 months had elapsed, the money was released because very few people left the business.

You may also find that there are parameters in place after the sale related to the business' performance. For example, if your business plan over three years shows growth, the acquirer will often agree to pay you more if the business achieves that level of growth after years one and two. This means, although you'll receive a large lump sum upfront on the sale of your business, there is also likely to be a steady stream of payments in the first few years after you exit.

Knowing when it's time to go

When you're planning an exit, potential acquirers will want to know whether the business needs you, the entrepreneur, or not at this juncture. They will want to see that you have a strong management team in place and that growth is not dependent on the entrepreneur.

In fact, in our experience the entrepreneur should aim to be "out" of the running of the business just before its growth peaks. Entrepreneurs have incredible energy and drive, but this can only be sustained for so long. Once your business reaches a certain point, growth has to be achieved in a different, equally sustainable way, which comes from having strong operational foundations and a strong management team in place.

If we take a football analogy, often you will see a good Championship side manager is able to get their team into the Premier League and usually they'll have a solid first season in the top flight. However, the second season is often where they come unstuck because the reality is that you need a different type of manager to generate sustained success under the pressure of the Premier League. In business the same principle often applies, in that many entrepreneurs have the skills to bring a business to a certain point on its journey, but then they need to step out at the right point to allow it to evolve to the next level.

We know it's easy to say, but it's much harder to have the self-awareness and maturity to recognise when your journey with a business is coming to an end and to know when it's time to hand that company over to someone else who has the ability to do more with it. It's important to recognise that, at some point, you will exit the business, even when you're seeking investment rather than actively planning for a sale.

Often it's the people around you who will help you realise when you've reached this point on your journey. You will likely see similar stories play out among the people you've hired throughout your time in your business. As we said in Chapter 3, there may be people you hire in the early days of your business who aren't suited to the same role as the business evolves and grows. People outgrow jobs and jobs outgrow people. We're sure you've seen this happen within your team and it's no different as the entrepreneur. The challenge is recognising where your skills in business lie and when it's your time to leave. This is often when the advice from an experienced non-exec can prove invaluable.

Negotiating your personal exit from the business

It's important to consider at what point you will leave the business after the sale, because often the acquirer will (sometimes financially) encourage you to stick around for a period of time after the sale goes through. Usually this is known as being in "golden handcuffs" or an "earn-out period". However, if you're an entrepreneur that has always run your own business, chances are that you'll struggle in a very corporate environment and may find it challenging to no longer be holding the reins of the business in the true sense of the word. You will more than likely also have set your sights on other things knowing that you will shortly be leaving this business. This means you want to negotiate your exit in as little time as possible. Acquirers usually understand this, hence agreeing to a short earn-out period.

What happens next?

Once you have got your head around walking away from your business, you then have to think about *how* this will manifest in your life. This can be more challenging than you might imagine, given that the majority of entrepreneurs (in our experience) work over 50 to 60 hours per week in their business and probably have done for more than a decade. You can't just switch that off because we just aren't geared that way. This means you have to plan your exit and think about how you want your life to look when you're not running the business any longer.

Each entrepreneur will use different tactics to manage their exit in a way that works for them. "I'd recommend not just stopping," Gary advises. "I've heard some pretty horrendous stories from people who have done that. When I exited my business, I did a lot of exercise and I stayed on the board so I could still keep my hand in. I also did a bit of consultancy work – I didn't just stop."

One of the most powerful concepts Gary learnt from The Strategic Coach® Program is retiring from what you *don't* want to do. However, it's important to consider what you *do* want to do with your newfound freedom. "I had no vision to become a mentor, chairman or investor," Gary reveals. "But it's been incredibly rewarding. There's less running around and doing, and more sharing and communicating. It's a whole new world and it's good!"

In fact, as Gary has discovered, one of the things most entrepreneurs work so hard for and crave is freedom, rather than money, a bigger house or a faster car. When you sell your business, you will have freedom with your time, money, purpose and relationships. You can very much do what you like and that is incredibly powerful. You also have to be mindful of what you do with your money, because even though you've made it that doesn't mean you will necessarily keep it if you have the wrong advisers around you or make poor decisions.

One of Guy's top tips for any entrepreneur that has just exited or is exiting their business is to take a bit of time out. "After the acquisition I took a year off and just pencilled nice things into my diary with my wife, my family and my friends," he says. "Largely that year was about doing things that freed my mind."

This is a particularly good opportunity to think about your freedom of purpose, what you want to do and how you can leave your mark on the world. What's your legacy going to be? What good things can you do that will get you out of bed in the morning? That might be setting up a new business, it might be acting as a non-exec director and sharing your experience with other entrepreneurs, or it might be investing in businesses that you see the value in. Speak to people in the entrepreneurial community and you'll be amazed at the opportunities that come your way. In fact, one of the hardest things is likely to be saying "No" to the multitude of opportunities that materialise.

We talked earlier about understanding where your skills as an entrepreneur lie and understanding this will also help you when you're looking for your purpose after you exit your business. For example, if you love taking a business through a period of fast growth, you can look for opportunities to do this again. It can become a phase you specialise in. Similarly there will be other people who specialise in professionalising and running much larger organisations. It's all about finding out where your passions lie.

"I'm pigeonholed in the £1-3 million EBITDA business when it comes to investing, because that's where I fly best. I'm comfortable there and it's what I enjoy the most," Gary explains. "This is when I can help transform a business and drive it to fast growth. I know this is what I do best. But I also know there are other people who prefer working in more mature businesses and others who love supporting startups."

Common pitfalls when exiting a business

There are a number of mistakes entrepreneurs can make when preparing to and then exiting their business, and we'll run through some of the most common here.

#1 Staying too long

We talked earlier in the chapter about how a business can evolve beyond the entrepreneur who started and grew it, and one of the biggest mistakes entrepreneurs make when exiting their businesses is staying too long. Interestingly, research published in the Harvard Business Review[2] revealed that four out of five CEOs are forced to step down from their post by their investors.

We understand how challenging it can be to relinquish control of your "baby" and leave it in the hands of others, but the fact is that when your business is acquired it's because you have done a great job of growing it and getting it in shape. However, the skills required to manage the business from this point are different to the skills that have got you this far. Rather than being forced out of your

---

2 Noam Wasserman, (2008), 'The Founder's Dilemma', *Harvard Business Review*, February, available at: https://hbr.org/2008/02/the-founders-dilemma

company, it's far better to negotiate your exit when you sell and go gracefully and on your own terms.

#2 Being derailed by unusual elements of due diligence

We talked in detail about the due diligence process in Chapter 5, but it's essential that you're prepared for some very strange things to come up during due diligence. In our experience, often the issues that will spook an investor are things you won't even have thought of. In many cases, this can be as the result of a survey by an independent expert, usually of a physical asset like a building. However, what you have to remember is that it's in the surveyor's interest to be very thorough. They don't want to miss anything because otherwise they could be liable in future. Our advice is to simply be prepared for what you might consider "non-issues" to crop up at this stage.

#3 Unpredictable market changes

We never know what is going to happen in the world, or within our industry. Look at the Covid-19 pandemic. The impact that had on businesses all over the world was monumental and certainly not something you would have been expecting at the start of 2020. Sometimes situations like this can completely derail an acquisition. For example, Guy reveals that an acquisition he was going through stalled completely in 2020, because the person leading the acquisition on the other side was furloughed during the pandemic and there hasn't been the confidence or bandwidth within that organisation to pick it back up.

#4 Overlooking the small print

This is more a pitfall that will hit after the acquisition, but it's very important to be aware of because it can affect the amount you receive for your business. In many cases, when you sell your business you'll receive an upfront payment and the remainder will be split over a period of years and will be conditional on your business achieving certain milestones. Often, this is a 60-40 split, with 60 per cent paid upfront and the remaining 40 per cent paid out over four years.

A problem can arise, however, should the organisation that's acquired your business then be acquired itself before those four years are up. If your legal team hasn't inserted caveats to protect your payments in the event that, through no fault of your own, you're unable to hit your targets, you stand to lose millions.

We can't stress enough how important it is to read all the small print, and for your lawyers to read all the small print, to ensure there aren't any hidden costs that will affect the amount you ultimately receive for your business.

#5 Failing to understand investment cycles

It's important to understand how investment cycles work and where your business fits into that particular cycle when you're seeking investment or being acquired. Generally speaking, private equity firms go out to raise funds and then have a set period of time during which to invest that capital and reap the rewards. This is typically a five plus two cycle. This means the private equity firm has five years to invest, get profits and then sell all their investments one year (or two if they take an extension) after that five years is up.

The challenge for an entrepreneur comes if you are acquired in year four of that five-year cycle, because that only gives you one year to turn the business around before the private equity firm sells you. What makes it more challenging is that private equity investors won't always tell you where you are in that cycle. This can land you in a lot of trouble, because at the end of their cycle the private equity firm will just tell you to raise the cash to give it back to their investors.

We have bought a company for much less than it was worth because it was in this precise situation. The entrepreneur and business was "underwater" and making no money, all because their investor was at the end of their cycle and just wanted to get them out of the door as quickly as possible. Since we acquired them, they have gone on to be very successful (which just highlights the point about choosing your investors wisely) but they made no money from that first investment.

Summary

Some of what we've discussed in this chapter might be new information to you and some of what we've shared around legal and shareholder agreements and pitfalls might make you question whether an acquisition is the right way to go. We've all seen how the Covid-19 pandemic has hit markets for at least two years and when events like that happen, there really is very little you can do except dust yourself off and get on with it.

What we'd like to remind you of is that you're an entrepreneur. That means you're creative, flexible and dynamic. If a problem comes up, whether it's a global pandemic or something else, the classic response from an entrepreneur is to pivot and ask, "What's going to make this work?". You will find solutions because ultimately that's what you get paid for, and this is exactly what any investor will want you to do too.

We'll leave you at the end of this chapter with a positive story about how one entrepreneur pivoted their business during the Covid-19 pandemic. This was an entrepreneur with a network of four coffee shops, that all had to close during lockdowns. Their response was to start selling coffee directly to people in their homes, because many of their customers had bought coffee machines and their habits had changed out of necessity. This particular business had a strong email list, pushed their offering on social media and, by the time all the lockdowns ended, the business was in a strong position.

That's just one story of many from this period, where entrepreneurs were forced to use all their problem-solving abilities to pivot and make the best of an unexpected and unprecedented situation. Of course, those pivots will have been made infinitely easier if your business has solid foundations and is well-run, so all of this ties in with not only seeing your business continue to grow and succeed, but also with you securing investment and eventually an exit from your business on your terms.

Fast-growth insights
When Guy started thinking about exiting his business, he had been running it for around 16 years and was wondering where it would end and what would happen

when it did. Alongside his board and senior team, he put together a three-year plan to maximise shareholder value in the business and lead to an exit.

This helped Guy to put his mindset in the right place for an exit, although he did go on an "emotional rollercoaster", as he describes it, when an offer came in and the process of selling the business began. This actually happened (unexpectedly!) not long after he had put his three-year exit plan in place. Guy and his shareholders discussed the offer, felt it was fair and were confident the business that had made it would honour the price they offered and not try to "chip" it down.

Having an exit strategy already in place allowed Guy to feel comfortable with his decision to exit the business at that stage. All this unexpected offer did was shorten the time frame of the process.

Part 4: Fast Forward...

CHAPTER NINE
INVESTING TRENDS

There are three main themes we're going to cover when it comes to the future of investing: technology (and the convergence of technology), the environment and corporate social responsibility (CSR).

The future is tech

There's no doubt in our minds that, for a business to survive and thrive in the next ten years, it needs to be a tech company or a tech-led company. When it comes to investment, tech and tech-led companies are the businesses that are attracting (at the time of writing) and that are likely to continue to attract the most interest and funding.

In the last chapter, we explained that a company's valuation is typically based on a multiple of its EBITDA, and that different industries have different multiple ranges. There is one exception to this: tech. Tech companies are valued based on a multiple of their revenue, rather than a multiple of their EBITDA.

At the time of writing, tech companies that deliver a service have valuations of between 0.8 and five times multiples of their revenues. Tech companies that deliver, for example, a subscription-based product and that have recurring revenues typically have valuations of between seven and

15 times their revenues. It's worth pointing out here that any business that can demonstrate recurring revenue will have a higher valuation than one that can't, but within the tech sector this equates to a substantially higher valuation.

If you have a tech business, investors (and eventual acquirers) want to see that you have consumers regularly and repeatedly using your service or product, and that you're continually improving your service through your products to keep the number of people who leave to a minimum.

You only have to look at what happened during the Covid-19 pandemic to see how perceptions of tech businesses are changing in the investing world. In years gone by, tech companies were often perceived to be outliers and almost a more risky investment. You might get a quick win if you put your money into tech, but you also had to accept you could lose. However, tech businesses are increasingly seen as the stable companies to invest in; you only have to look at the top Fortune 500 companies to see this trend.

In fact, most of the companies on that list now are not the same ones you would have found if you'd looked at it 20 or 30 years ago. Oil companies, while still present, are a good example of where industries are falling out of favour. These businesses are gradually slipping down the list and their valuations are considerably lower than tech-led companies (at the time of writing typically between two and four times EBITDA).

Essentially, those multiples reflect the future of investing and are a good indication of where investors and therefore businesses are going.

Even if you aren't what would be classed as a technology business, you still need to be tech-led within your sector. That means using the latest tools available to run your business and sell your services or products. Gary recollects that one of his businesses built its own land reservation system, using the latest technology to give them the edge. "You have to go towards technology, no matter what industry you operate in, because that's where the margins are," he explains.

At this stage, you either have to be a tech business or a tech-led business, otherwise you simply won't be around in ten years' time. All the smart money is going into these kinds of businesses at the moment. *The Future Is Faster Than You Think*[3] is a book by futurists Peter Diamandis and Steven Kotler that explores how the convergence of technology is transforming not only business, but also our lives.

3 Peter Diamandis and Steven Kotler, (2020), 'The Future Is Faster Than You Think: How Converging Technologies Are Transforming Business, Industries and Our Lives', *Simon & Schuster*, 1st edition

The authors predict that, in the next decade, we will experience more change than we have in the last century. All of this change will be driven by technology.

However, there is also a lot of smoke and mirrors surrounding tech-based businesses at the time of writing. The term AI gets used by a lot of companies, and not always correctly. Some businesses have recognised that AI is what investors want to hear, so they use the term but aren't necessarily using AI in their companies. If that's the case, they will get found out eventually. We wouldn't actually be surprised if something similar to the dot com bubble happens in this space in the coming years as due diligence on the technology side becomes more sophisticated, allowing investors and acquirers to more easily spot the businesses genuinely harnessing AI from those that don't.

The convergence of technology

In addition to this rapidly growing appetite for tech and tech-led businesses, there is also a convergence of technology occurring. This is where technology and other sectors converge to change the way we do things (something we'll look at further when we talk about environmental investing). The emergence of 5G is going to be particularly important, because of the significant bandwidth 5G provides for wireless and mobile data transfer.

When you combine 5G with another emerging technology like AI there are opportunities to transform our lives. For example, just imagine that a medical scanner takes an image of someone's lungs and AI is able to identify, with a 99 per cent rate of success, whether that person has cancer. What's more, that scan could be carried out in the UK, but the AI technology could be in America and the scan and results could be sent back in a matter of minutes. This is just one example of how technology can converge and change the way we work in many different industries.

The future is green

The green agenda is another area that is hugely important for the future of investing. Environmental credentials within businesses are being scrutinised more and more closely and businesses that "greenwash" will be found out and likely suffer as a result.

There are also examples of how the convergence of technology and the green agenda combine, showing how these strands combine. For example, Robert Piconi, CEO and cofounder of Energy Vault, has explained that he's exploring alternative renewable energy technology because there are so few places left around the world that are suitable for hydroelectric plants to be developed. Hydroelectric power is incredibly cheap to produce, because the water that powers the turbines (and in doing so generates energy) flows downhill naturally.

He looked at this process and found a way to replicate it so that you can produce energy at night and in doing so "store" the power that's produced during the day. The system he came up with involved a crane, a turbine, solar power and concrete blocks. Essentially, the crane would use solar energy generated during the day to turn the motor that lifted these concrete blocks up. Then at night, when there is no solar energy being produced, these blocks would be let down slowly, thereby driving the turbine and generating power. It is, in effect, a way to store renewable energy and put it back into the grid when it's needed[4]. This is just one of many examples of how bright entrepreneurs are using innovative technology to solve problems in the world of green energy.

The future is responsible

The other major trend when it comes to growing businesses and investing is corporate social responsibility (CSR). In the past, being socially responsible was seen as a bonus

4 Matt Reynolds, (2022), 'Gravity Could Solve Clean Energy's One Major Drawback', *Wired*, 4 January, available at: https://www.wired.co.uk/article/energy-vault-gravity-storage

for your business, rather than a necessity, but nowadays if you aren't strong with your CSR practises you will struggle to attract talent and, even if you manage to attract them, you won't retain them.

Customers will, quite rightly, also crucify you if you're not behaving responsibly, doing the right thing and following accepted good practices in this area. There are countless examples of businesses that have experienced challenges as a result of poor behaviour in this area and the reason it's so important for you as you're seeking investment or looking to exit your business is that it affects share prices.

Having a properly laid out CSR agenda, as well as a green agenda, is a necessity for your business. If you look just at publicly listed companies and how investments work in that realm of business, you can see that some of the biggest investment players already have sustainable funds and they rule businesses in or out based on how they perform environmentally and in relation to CSR. As people's awareness of the need for greater social responsibility increases, which is already happening rapidly, businesses will need to meet those criteria and follow good practice if they want to get investment. Share prices are affected by how you perform in these areas.

You only have to look at how consumer behaviour has shifted in recent years on a very basic level to see how this ripples out into entire businesses. Guy reveals that, for example, he's switched to driving a Tesla electric car, which means he's no longer relying on fossil fuels for transport or creating air pollution as he drives around. That may only seem like a relatively small thing to change, but people care about these things and as consumer habits change, business models need to as well. As people become more socially responsible in their everyday lives and choices, businesses will need to adapt to become more socially responsible themselves, if they aren't already.

This has to be on every corporate agenda and it has to be part of your business plan whether you're a startup, a small business aiming for fast growth or a privately owned company that's preparing to look for investment. Investors are increasingly looking for strong CSR and green credentials in the businesses they invest in and, as we've said, these factors affect the value of a business which will ultimately mean if you don't do these things (and do them well) you will lose out when you eventually exit your business.

Leading the way in a new world

All of these factors have an impact on leadership and the traits needed to successfully lead businesses of every size. CSR, equality, diversity and inclusion and the environment are all areas where you, as a CEO, need to show leadership and not just pay lip service to these agendas. How you communicate and engage with people around these areas has become critical to business success.

There are many examples of people in leadership positions making poorly thought out or insensitive comments, and both them and their businesses paying the price for that. You really can't afford to get this wrong.

Similarly, you need to think very carefully about what you post and share on social media, because investors and potential acquirers will look at your social media profiles. We've all seen the stories of sports people, for instance, who have posted something when they were young and didn't think through the consequences, only for this to resurface ten or 15 years later and cause them all kinds of problems.

The same is true in the world of business; even if it doesn't get splashed all over the tabloids it will certainly find its way in front of your potential investors or acquirers. As a business, you will more than likely vet prospective employees' social media before you offer them a position to make sure there isn't anything that could cause reputational damage to your business. Investors will do the same when they are deciding whether you put money into your company.

If, as you're reading this, you're realising there might be some ill-advised posts from your youth online or even poorly chosen posts associated with your company, the worst thing you can do is try to hide them from potential investors. It is far better to be open and honest, raise the problem early, explain it (if there is an explanation) and hope that you can all move on.

This all comes back to leadership and making sure that you are leading the company from the front. You want to not only say all the right things, but to be doing them too, both personally and within your business.

Summary

We've highlighted the three main areas that we believe will increasingly be what investors focus on: technology and tech-led businesses, the environment and business' green agendas, and CSR practices. Weaving through all of these is the thread of the convergence of technology and how this will transform businesses and our everyday lives in the future.

Whatever stage you are at on your entrepreneurial journey, you would do well to consider how your company fares in each of these areas and to look at how you can improve in all of them if you want to give your business the best chance of achieving fast growth and finding investment in the future.

Part 4: Fast Forward...

CHAPTER TEN
THRIVING IN
A RECESSION

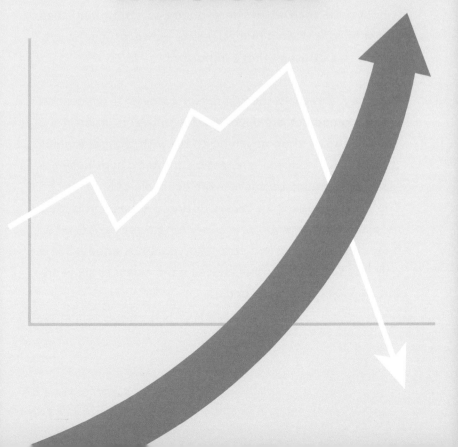

When you hear the "R" word (recession) does it strike fear into your heart, or are you rolling up your sleeves and looking for opportunities to capitalise on an economic downturn? Many businesses, big and small, feel as though they need to hold onto their cash and hunker down in a recession.

While understandable, we don't believe this is the right approach if you have ambitions of achieving fast growth; we'd encourage you to tune into your entrepreneurial mindset and spot the opportunities a recession presents.

Arguably, Warren Buffett is the master of finding opportunities during a recession. His strategy is simple – hold onto cash when the economy is strong and then invest billions when a recession hits. However, it's the *why* behind this strategy that's important.

This "why" is twofold: the first reason to invest in a recession is that companies are devalued due to the situation in the market, rather than anything to do with the companies themselves. In essence, a recession creates a huge business "sale", where good businesses are available at lower prices. The second reason to invest during a recession is that recessions are temporary. Every single recession we've been through in the last 100–150 years has ended. Some only last six months, others have lasted closer to six years. But they all come to an end.

If acquiring other companies to support your growth is part of your plan, a recession could be the ideal time to start shopping, because you will find good businesses are available at much lower prices than during times of economic growth.

A good company is still a good company, even if a recession hits – it doesn't become "bad" overnight due to the external environment in which it operates taking a downturn. If you're positioning your business for fast growth, a recession won't affect the amazing products or services you provide. It is merely a temporary change in your environment and, in fact, one that has the potential to accelerate your success.

Master your mindset

Developing a truly entrepreneurial mindset, as we discussed in Part 1, is crucial if you want to capitalise on the opportunities a recession presents. The mainstream media is very good at presenting a "doom and gloom" picture of the state of the economy and it can take a great deal of mental strength to see past this and remain optimistic and focused on your growth plans.

This mental strength and mindset is what sets fast-growth businesses apart from their counterparts. The Covid-19 pandemic in particular highlighted how identifying opportunities to diversify not only allowed businesses to continue operating in a period of incredible upheaval, but also enabled them to grow.

Coffee shops are a fantastic example. When the UK went into lockdown, all coffee shops had to close. Their normal stream of income – people picking up a cup of coffee – vanished overnight. However, the coffee shops' customers still wanted their coffee, they just weren't able to buy it in the same way they used to.

The coffee shop owners with entrepreneurial mindsets realised that they still had opportunities to serve their customers, but that they would have to think differently. The smart ones started selling coffee beans through a delivery service. Some sold coffee machines. The really smart ones offered this as a subscription service to create a recurring revenue stream.

In doing so, they not only survived successive Covid-related lockdowns but also their businesses emerged from the disruption of the pandemic stronger than they were before, because they had added another stream of revenue to the business. People could pop into the coffee shop for their morning caffeine hit, or they could have their coffee beans delivered to their door. Some of their customers now use both services.

Other businesses pivoted their offering to suit the unprecedented situation in which we found ourselves. Gin makers are a great example of this. While they could still sell gin through supermarkets and off-licences, some decided to explore how they could expand their business. They took it back to basics by asking how else alcohol is used; the answer – as the base ingredient for hand sanitiser. During the Covid-19 pandemic, everyone wanted hand sanitiser. The smart gin makers capitalised on this and started manufacturing this product alongside their standard offering.

These are just two examples of good business news that came out of the Covid-19 pandemic, and they are two of many. Whenever you start to feel as though you're being dragged down by the negative headlines, remember that they are not representative of all the good and innovative things happening in the world – there are many bright people out there who are working to make the world a better place. They might not make the evening news, but they are out there making a difference.

We have seen our fair share of recessions over the decades that we've been in business and we can tell you with confidence that there are good opportunities in every bad situation, you just have to look for them and develop a filter to block out the negative news that we're surrounded by.

Guy started his tech business in 2001, at the end of the dot-com boom, which was arguably the worst-possible time to start a tech business. However, his company made money and grew every single year, despite the challenging economic conditions at the start, and another recession in 2008–09. How did Guy manage that when businesses around him were folding? By having the right mindset and adapting to the situation.

Be part of the right communities

Gary and Guy are both members of the the Strategic Coach® program, and they both state that this community has been instrumental in helping them achieve what they have throughout their careers.

One of the keys to avoiding hitting the panic button in economic downturns, especially when you are relatively new as an entrepreneur, is surrounding yourself with good people who take a positive approach to business. We only ever talk about recessions as offering opportunities – we never mention them in negative terms.

Learning to switch off the news can be challenging, but it is well worth it. We strongly recommend joining a community of like-minded entrepreneurs, because they will give you the confidence to do what needs to be done during tough times, and to come out the other side of those challenges fighting and stronger than your competitors.

Spend on marketing to see results

As we said at the start of this chapter, many businesses hunker down, spend less money and maybe even make redundancies to reel in costs during a recession. In many companies, the marketing budget is one of the first things that gets cut.

But if you look at the companies that come out of a recession ahead of their competitors, you'll almost always see that they have *increased* their marketing spend during a recession. The reason for doing so is simple: there is less noise in the marketplace during a recession and, as a result, anything you do put out will be multiplied. Those people who are looking to spend money during this time will come to you, because you're visible.

When the recession ends (which it always will), you're in a really strong position to capitalise on businesses that are ready to spend again. By keeping up with your marketing, or even increasing it, you're putting yourself streets ahead of all the businesses that hunkered down and cut their marketing spend during the same period.

Putting yourself out there through marketing during a recession also has the effect of showing the world that you're growing, despite the challenging economic circumstances. This means you'll be perceived as a strong company, one that can weather economic storms, and are therefore a safe bet for investment (both from investors and from clients who want to trust you to provide them with services through thick and thin).

The same is true of almost any spending during a recession, whether we're talking about sales, capital spending or real estate investment.

Of course, choosing when and what to spend money on is not always solely your decision as an entrepreneur. You need to have a strong board – and strong investors – who share your mindset and therefore support and understand your strategy of amplifying your presence during a recession to accelerate your growth.

Seek out acquisitions

If you have the cash reserves available, a recession is the ideal time to look for acquisitions, because as we said at the beginning of this chapter, many good businesses will be devalued, even though the change is in the external environment, rather than within the business itself.

What that means for you and your business is that you could acquire a complementary company, that supports and accelerates your growth, for a very good price. Not every business will be in a position to acquire during a recession, and many businesses won't be looking for acquisitions at all, and that's fine. However, if acquiring other companies is already part of your fast-growth strategy, a recession is the perfect time to look around and see what you can find.

Investors will do the same for precisely this reason – they know they can pick up good, strong companies for lower prices than they would in a stronger market.

Know your value

Because investors understand that they can pick up good companies at lower prices, this may mean you are approached by potential investors during a recession. Experienced investors know they can acquire or invest in businesses during an economic downturn and get them ready to come out of this cycle stronger than ever.

However, it's important to consider whether now is the right time for you to take on investment – do you really need it at this stage? Gary actually turned down investment opportunities during the Covid-19 pandemic because he could see it wasn't the right option for the entrepreneurs in question.

"I had about ten companies coming to me seeking investment during the Covid-19 pandemic, and I actually talked them out of it," Gary recalls. "One entrepreneur in particular offered me 25 per cent of his company, which was a great company before Covid, but during the pandemic he lost his bottle a little bit and felt as though he needed to go out and find some cash."

So, what did he say? "I took him back to basics and explained he had a great business," Gary reveals. "I pointed out that he was eligible for a loan of between £60,000–£80,000 from the government, and he wouldn't have to give them any shares in return. In the end, that's exactly what he did. He kept all his shares and, surprise, surprise, he's in great shape now."

Not every business owner will be lucky enough to speak to an investor like Gary though. This is why it's important, firstly, not to panic and to view the situation logically. As Gary says, go back to basics and look at the facts of your business and its performance – if it was strong before a recession, then it's highly likely to remain strong during a recession. Secondly, it highlights the importance of considering all your options when you are seeking funding.

If you are seeking investment during a recession (and even when you're not), you have to be realistic about the valuation you are aiming for. While it's true that a good company is a good company regardless of the economic circumstances, the risk of investing is perceived to be higher during a recession. Be mindful of this and make sure you are not asking for too much from your investors, because they will walk away if they believe your valuation is unrealistic.

Find the right funding option for your business

We will freely admit that it can be a tad harder to raise money during a recession. Mainstream banks will simply pull up their drawbridges and refuse to lend, or put their rates right up. Neither of which will help you if you're seeking investment.

Similarly, corporate investors also tend to be a bit more conservative during a recession and will be more likely to spend money on their existing portfolio than to bring new investments into their portfolio during this time.

However, losing access to mainstream funding can be an opportunity in itself. This encourages you to look for other sources of funds, of which the best option is usually private investors, particularly for early-stage entrepreneurs.

There is a caveat to this – private investors will usually want a slightly higher rate of return than the interest rate you'd pay through a standard lender, and with good reason. They could put their capital into a safe investment account with a mainstream bank instead of giving it to you, which carries greater risk. Therefore the return you offer has to outweigh what they could receive from more traditional products.

Rather than focus on how much it will cost you, though, flip the equation so you focus on what the investment will mean for the business. If funds from a private investor will accelerate your business growth and propel you forwards then it is worth paying a little more to access them during periods when mainstream lenders are battening down the hatches.

You might think that, because it's going to be more expensive to raise money during a recession, you're better off riding it out without the investment and trying again when the economic situation changes. However, remember that there are different ways in which to raise funding.

You could approach angel investors or successful entrepreneurs, who understand where you're coming from, for a smaller investment designed to tide you over until the end of the recession. Often such investors will provide you with money at a reasonable rate.

Or the higher rates on borrowing might mean that, rather than trying to raise multi-millions through Series A funding, you instead explore a bridging round. This will allow you to secure funding at a lower level to see you through this period, and once the economic situation improves you can go for Series A funding.

This approach will actually put you in an even stronger position when you do seek that funding too, because your business will demonstrate growth during a period when many naysayers would have expected you to shrink. This means you are likely to be offered a better Series A rate from an equity point of view than you would have if you'd sought this funding earlier in your journey.

Turn these challenges around and think about how you can use the situation to your advantage – and how a change of tack now could pave the way for even faster growth in the future.

Find the right investors

Equally as important as finding the right funding option is finding the right investors for your business. We've talked about this extensively earlier in the book, but this is particularly paramount during a recession because you will likely demand more from your investors during challenging times.

Finding the right investors hinges on how well you can portray your business proposition and on the relationship you can build with your investors. As we've said throughout this book, the right investor will provide far more than just financial support, and you may need to lean on their experience and knowledge more in challenging economic times than you do when the economy is booming.

Understandably, investors will scrutinise the numbers behind any business they are considering funding, and this is especially the case in times of recession. This means it is worth spending additional time finessing your figures to ensure they can withstand that scrutiny. The key is knowing what amount you genuinely need to support your business growth. What you have to avoid at all costs is fattening your numbers, because prospective investors will notice and they won't invest.

The figures you produce have to tell the same story as your pitch deck and in challenging economic periods it's more important than ever that your figures and your pitch deck story correlate.

If this is an area you are struggling with, you could ask financially minded friends or family members for their thoughts on whether what you are saying in your pitch aligns and makes sense from a financial perspective. Sometimes an outside perspective can be invaluable.

Take advantage of the recession

When you're putting together a pitch deck, don't shy away from the fact that the economy is entering or is already in a recession. Lean into it and explain how your business is going to take advantage of the recession. Investors will sit up and listen if you can show that you've not only thought about how you're going to trade during what is likely to be a difficult 12–18 months, but that you've also got a plan to capitalise on it and set yourself up for future success.

If you have a product that will help other businesses reduce their costs, a recession is the time to shout about it. Sales generation can be challenging in a recession, but if what you're offering will help others lower their outgoings then an economic downturn can be extremely advantageous because your product will almost sell itself.

Summary

Hopefully, you are no longer seeing a recession as something scary but, in fact, as a period in time that can offer incredible opportunities if you just look for them. We have highlighted various ways in which you can seize opportunities during a recession throughout this chapter, but undoubtedly the most important is having the right mindset to do so.

Surrounding yourself with other people who see the advantages in recessions, rather than those who get sucked into the negative news spiral, will really help you retain clarity of thought and avoid panicking when the economy takes a dip.

When your mindset is primed for seeing opportunities, you will view the situation differently and, as a result, start seeing creative solutions where others only see problems. This might be in the form of a new product or service you can offer existing customers, or an innovative method of funding that can see you through a period when traditional borrowing is harder to access.

There are many ways in which you can take advantage of a recession in your business, and even use it to accelerate your journey towards fast growth.

Fast-growth insights

During the 2007–08 recession, Gary was faced with a potentially serious problem – he needed to raise millions of pounds to build on a series of plots he'd invested in, but access to mainstream sources of funding had been cut off.

Prior to the recession, each plot had been valued at £50,000 but, when the recession hit, Gary was told their value was £0 because he wouldn't be able to source the bank debt to fund building on the land.

Not one to give up, Gary and his team found a private investor who agreed to provide the capital they needed and received 10 per cent on the millions they put into the business in return. This enabled Gary to carry out the building work and, as a result, build a highly successful business that is still going strong more than 15 years later.

CONCLUSION

We sincerely hope that, having reached the end of this book, you feel more confident about the prospect of seeking investment for your business. Perhaps what you have read here has highlighted some areas of your business that you need to work on; or maybe reading these chapters has shown you that you are closer to being ready to seek investment and push for fast growth than you realised. Either way, if you follow the advice we have shared, based on our collective decades of experience as both entrepreneurs and investors, you will be well-placed whatever course your business takes.

If nothing else, we hope that we have demystified the process of seeking investment. There is no denying that setting your business on a fast-growth trajectory takes work and requires blood, sweat and tears (not necessarily literally) from you as the entrepreneur, as well as investment. However, with the right investor and support around you, this process can be made much less painful.

This is precisely why we established EHE Group, because we wanted to take some of the pain out of the process of seeking investment, match entrepreneurs with the right selection of investors for their business and create a community which helps entrepreneurs to grow. . It is just as beneficial for investors to build relationships with entrepreneurs they align with, making our approach to investment win-win.

If, after reading this book, you would like to explore your investment options and receive some guidance from experienced entrepreneurs who have been there, done that and got the T-shirt, please contact us via our website: https://www.ehe.capital/. We are always excited to hear from ambitious entrepreneurs with exciting and unique businesses, whether you are at the startup stage or well-established and looking to propel your organisation towards fast growth.

We believe that, with the right investment and support, entrepreneurs can achieve the extraordinary. We look forward to welcoming you to the EHE Community.

THE ENTREPRENEUR'S DICTIONARY

The following are terms that you will hear and need to know when you start seeking investment. The problem is, often no one tells you what these are or what they mean before you get started. We've included a general definition, followed by an explanation of what you, as an entrepreneur, need to know. Hopefully the following definitions will mean you're never left sitting in a meeting with investors wondering what on Earth they're talking about...

Add-on acquisition (Bolt on)

When a "platform company" acquires another company to help that original company grow.

EHE insight: This is about buying another company that complements yours. Normally these types of acquisitions either increase bottom-line profits by saving overheads/central costs or help the original company grow by giving it greater geographical reach, an increased product range or more customers. Add-on acquisitions are a great way of growing more quickly than you can through organic growth.

Angel investor

A high-net-worth person who invests directly in startup companies in exchange for equity.

EHE insight: These are the gold dust of the investing world. They are great if you can find them, but really rare. Angel investors are very useful to bring onboard in the early stages of your company because they will back you, they understand growth and they offer fewer barriers to investment than institutions. An angel investor won't want to dive into your data room, they will just need specific information. Often they will take a greater risk than an institution will. Your relationship with an angel investor will often be less formal than with an institution too.

Asset-backed lending

A type of lending that is secured by assets held by the borrowing company, i.e. secured on property, inventory, equipment or even accounts receivable.

EHE insight: This is a cheap form of lending which should attract low interest rates as the lender has first charge on the company's assets, thereby reducing their risk. If you have assets in your business, this is a good option.

Buyout

Where an investor acquires control of a mature, operating company.

EHE insight: As well as one company buying out another, you can also have management buyouts (MBOs). MBOs typically happen when a manager decides they want to retire, they have a strong management team in place and that team decides to "buy out" the retiring manager. Nearly all buyouts will involve as much bank debt as possible because this is the cheapest form of loan (at the time of writing typically three to six per cent per annum), whereas equity investment is more expensive (typically ten to 30 per cent per annum). Just remember that the reason bank debt is cheap is because the bank gets paid out first!

Capital gains

The difference between an asset's purchase price and sale price. Capital gains is taxed at a lower rate than other forms of income tax.

EHE insight: Capital gains will be relevant when you sell the company. Capital gains tax (CGT) is charged at 20 per cent and is the payment you'll make to HMRC (although you may be eligible for business asset disposal relief when you sell your business to reduce this figure).

CAP Table (Capitalisation)

A table or spreadsheet showing the ownership of the company.

EHE insight: This is essentially a list of who owns what in your business. It will show loan notes, equity and who has any preference in payment and in what order (see alphabet shares). If you're bringing in an investor, you need to pay close attention to this because your CAP Table sets out the structure of how the investor sees things going forward. Investors want to see a business' CAP Table because it will help them work out how much equity is available and how they can best structure their investment in your company. Make sure you ask to see the CAP Table your investor sets out if they don't readily share it with you, so you can check you're happy with the new ownership structure that is being proposed.

Club deal

When more than one investor clubs together to finance the acquisition of the company.

EHE insight: Essentially you're dealing with more than one investor because one investor does not have enough firepower to do the deal on their own (a bit like only being able to afford the sandwich in a meal deal and needing to borrow money from your mate to cover the drink and snack). Approach club deals with caution and be aware that because one investor can't quite afford it themselves, they will need to bring someone else in. This can be advantageous because it will mean you have different investors with different skills backing you. However, the downside can come if you want to complete add-on acquisitions, as the investor may not be able to stretch to these if they've gone to their maximum to get the deal with you. This all needs to be agreed upfront so there are no surprises. As you get higher up the food chain in value terms, banks have been known to agree to club deals if the loan amount exceeds their comfort level in a particular sector.

Data room

A web-based secure depository of digital information, often relating to due diligence on a company.

EHE insight: This is a place we recommend entrepreneurs avoid! It contains hundreds of pages of documents that will provide more information than you'll ever need. However, a data room is critical for directors, project managers and advisers (e.g. accountants and legal teams). Your team will need to deposit documents here if you're seeking investment or being acquired. If you are acquiring another business, your team will need to enter their data room.

Setting up a virtual data room means your team won't be fielding multiple requests for the same documents from various people during the process.

Drag along and tag along rights

Drag along rights enable the investor/preferred shareholder to force others to go along with the sale of the company. With tag along rights, the investor may want to sell shares/company and the co-holders of tag along rights can participate in the sale.

EHE insight: A legal term that most investors will look at and want to action. You need to decide whether you want to agree to this or not upfront. While you will likely be aligned to maximise shareholder value, on the edges that can vary. On many occasions a sale will be mutually beneficial, but on some occasions a sale could put your equity value at stake.

Due diligence

Also known as DD for short. It's the process undertaken by a potential investor, often using third-party experts, to analyse the different areas of the business.

EHE insight: *Often a painful process for entrepreneurs (the phrase "death by analysts" springs to mind!). At the point that you grant an investor exclusivity, they will crawl all over your business checking everything from the finances, commercial and insurance to IT, legal titles and management. If they find anything negative, this will affect the price they offer.*

EBITDA (Earnings Before Interest, Taxes, Depreciation & Amortisation)

This is a common metric for buyout valuations, which are usually calculated as a multiple of a company's EBITDA.

EHE insight: *Eeebit-Dah is a word to get to know and use frequently when discussing your business with investors! Simply, it is a word for profit. Your company will be valued as a multiple of its EBITDA. For example, oil and gas companies might have a valuation of 4-6 x EBITDA, while hotels may have a valuation of 10-14 x EBITDA. Interestingly, tech companies are something of an anomaly, as they are usually valued as multiples of their turnover, rather than EBITDA.*

Entrepreneur/management warranties

A seller's assurance to a purchaser that the goods or services being purchased are (or shall be) as represented and, if not, will be replaced or repaired. Warranties for your goods and services can be either express or implied.

EV (Enterprise Value)

EV is a measure of a company's total value, often used as a more comprehensive alternative to equity market capitalisation. Enterprise value includes in its calculation the market capitalisation of a company, as well as short-term and long-term debt and any cash on the company's balance sheet.

EHE insight: This is a term you'll hear a lot. Essentially it's the value of the business after you have paid back any bank debt and loan notes. It's what you'll have to share between you once those debts are cleared.

Exclusivity agreement

Also known as lock-out, shut-out or no-shop agreements. These agreements are used to try to ensure that the other party to a prospective deal negotiates solely with the client for a period of time. They aim to give the client some protection from another party outbidding them.

EHE insight: See exclusivity period.

Exclusivity period

The period of time when you and the investor agree that they have to carry out the due diligence and complete the deal. Extensions can be, and are, agreed with both parties' consent.

EHE insight: This period usually lasts eight to 12 weeks once you have whittled down all those looking to invest in your business to your preferred investor. During DD, the investor is paying hard cash to their advisers. Often they will stagger and sequence the DD process so that the least expensive bits are completed first, building up to the expensive legal fees, as this allows them to pull out with minimum expense if they find something untoward. If both parties fail to agree terms at the end of this period, you are free to go to another investor. It's really important that you have a back-up investor who you keep warm during this time, so that if your preferred investor pulls out you have another option. This is also advisable because investors will often bring up "crunch" issues late in the exclusivity period in the hope of chipping the price down.

Exit

The act of realising an investment.

EHE insight: This should be the absolute focus of the entrepreneur and the investor. You both need to be completely aligned about what an exit looks and feels like. Strongly or loosely defined exits should be discussed at the outset. Cover variables such as market, sector sentiment, which company or investor is the next buyer and how you can make your company attractive to them. This is critical for realising the full value of your business.

Investor charges/fees

These charges can be wide and varied. They are also called transaction fees, deal fees, annual charges, management charges and other terms.

EHE insight: You often won't learn what these are until late in the process, as it usually doesn't come up in LOIs or term sheets. However, it's important that you know what fees you're going to pay as part of getting this investor on board. The key ones to look out for and agree upfront are the deal fees. Not only do investors/ PE companies charge their own investors management fees, they also charge the target company (aka your business) fees. Often this is a percentage of the size of the investment, such as one to two per cent. On a £30 million investment, this would amount to £600,000 as a one-off payment (although watch out for any exit fees too!). Ongoing management fees can also be levied on a target company per annum, often to cover and contribute to the investors'/PE company's overheads. Again, these can be a fixed sum or a percentage.

Investor's money often also carries an annual coupon (the interest rate can be anywhere from six to 12 per cent pa) which is termed "loan notes". The interest on loan notes is applied annually but only paid at the end of the investment when the company is sold. Loan notes rank lower than bank debt but higher than equity.

IPO (Initial Public Offering)

The first time a company sells its stock to the public. It can have an AIM or full stock market listing, depending on the size of the company. This is also known as "floating" a company.

EHE insight: An AIM listing is for companies at the smaller end of the scale (typically a minimum of £10 million EBITDA is required to be considered for an AIM listing). Larger companies can make an IPO on the full stock market. If you are aiming for an IPO, you as the entrepreneur will almost certainly need to be replaced, because most entrepreneurs don't do well with the public market bureaucracy and red tape! Be aware of this and replace yourself at least a year, if not 18 months, out from the IPO. The management team will need to be a bit more corporate because the market will want to see stability in the company and have confidence they can execute. An IPO is a great exit for a company as good returns are typically obtained.

IRR (Internal Rate of Return)

An annualised rate of return from a series of cash flows relating to a fund that can be gross or net.

EHE insight: Most entrepreneurs don't need to worry about IRR (which is investor speak). Instead, focus on driving EBITDA, growth and exit multiples/values and leave IRR to the accountants!

Key person

The most important person managing the investment or managing the company.

EHE insight: Key person insurance is often required if the entrepreneur is critical to the business' success. It pays out if the key person becomes ill and can no longer run the business.

KPI (Key Performance Indicator)

KPIs are measurable values used to evaluate how successful a person or organisation is at reaching a target. You can have high-level KPIs that look at the performance of your business, or KPIs that drill down into processes at the individual or departmental level.

EHE insight: We have no doubt that you're familiar with KPIs (and if you're not, you should be!)

LOI (Letter of Intent)

An LOI (which is similar to heads of terms or a term sheet) describes the principal terms of the investment.

EHE insight: An LOI is often useful because it is written in plain English and sets out the terms of the deal before it's passed to the lawyers. It's worth spending time on an LOI and agreeing it with your investor, fleshing out the terms at this stage rather than waiting until further down the line.

Management fee

This is often charged by an investor to manage the day-to-day of the fund. It is typically a charge of two per cent of the committed capital each year during the investment period.

EHE insight: This management fee is charged to the investor's investors. It is sometimes described as two and 20, which means the PE firm charges investors two per cent per annum and 20 per cent of the value created in the fund. For example, a private investor puts £30 million in a fund, hoping to get a £90 million return over five plus two years. If it takes the full seven years, the private investor is charged two per cent per annum on their £30 million, plus 20 per cent on the £60 million return created. This is how PE companies make their money – in this example they earn £12 million plus £600,000 per annum.

Mezzanine finance

Also called Mez debt. It is often used in deals and is a form of debt financing that shares many characteristics with equity financing. Mez debt is junior (subordinate) to a company's senior bank debt, but is senior to all loan notes and equity.

EHE insight: Mez debt is a very useful midway finance position between senior bank debt and equity if there is a funding gap. There are many specialist mez funds in the marketplace, including some banks. Because it is junior to bank debt, it is considered a bit more risky and therefore costs a bit more (so if senior bank debt has an interest rate of four per cent, mez debt will likely carry a rate of eight to ten per cent).

NDA (Non-Disclosure Agreement)

A non-disclosure agreement is a legally binding contract that establishes a confidential relationship. The party or parties signing the agreement agree that any sensitive information they may obtain will not be made available to any others. An NDA may also be referred to as a confidentiality agreement.

EHE insight: We're sure you're familiar with these!

Non executive

A non executive can be a director or chairperson (NXD/ NXC) who is a member of the board but not an employee nor part of the executive management team.

EHE insight: Non executives can be critical to your success. They have "been there and done it", which means they can be a valuable mentor to help develop you and the business. They are often rewarded with monthly fees and a small amount of equity, to align themselves with both executive and investor.

Pari passu

A way to ensure equal treatment between investors and entrepreneurs for dividends, exit funds and waterfall payments.

EHE insight: This is an important negotiating term to use with your investors. However, just because you have pari passu in one area of the deal, don't assume that's the case in others! Each point will be negotiated separately.

Pitch and pitch deck

A pitch is a meeting with, in this context, investors where entrepreneurs present their idea, concept and business plan. The pitch deck is a presentation deck that's used to pitch your idea or company to any number of audiences, generally investors.

EHE insight: Read Chapter 7 (if you haven't already!)

Pre-money valuation

A pre-money valuation refers to the value of a company before it goes public or receives other investments such as external funding or financing.

EHE insight: This is the value that's applied to a company before it's had any investment and in some cases before it's started trading. It's most commonly used in tech companies. As an example, if an investor puts £500,000 into a business with a pre-money valuation of £5 million, they will receive ten per cent of the shares.

Private equity (PE) fund/investor cycles

A PE fund will go through four stages, often over five years, plus a further two-year period (some can also be 10 years plus two years). The first phase is formation, where the PE company goes out and raises its funds from individuals or institutions. The second phase is investment, where the fund invests most of the capital it has raised into buying companies. The third phase is harvesting, when the fund starts to sell its companies and realise its profits. The final phase is an extension of one or two years, giving the fund time to exit companies which are not on track before they pay back their own investors.

EHE insight: *It's important that you're aware of where the investor is in their funding cycle (you may have to dig around a bit to find this information). Why is this important? Look back at the pitfalls of exiting a business in Chapter 8 – if you obtain investment towards the end of a PE funding cycle, you may not have the time you need to deliver the growth you are planning. If the investor has included drag along rights in your agreement, you could find yourself being forced to sell the company before you've obtained its full value.*

Seed stage

Pre-seed and seed funding are the earliest stages of funding which helps a startup grow. When you're in the midst of developing a startup, among the most important elements of creating a company is to obtain funding that will assist with development.

EHE insight: *At this stage, you are far better off trying to source non-equity funding, such as through friends and family.*

Series A financing

Series A financing refers to an investment in a privately-held, startup company after it has shown progress in building its business model and demonstrates the potential to grow and generate revenue.

EHE insight: There are a number of groups and associations (like EHE Group) that have connections to a number of investors and angel investors that can make the process of finding this type of funding much easier.

Series B funding

Series B rounds are all about taking businesses to the next level, past the development stage. Investors help startups get there by expanding market reach. Companies that have gone through seed and Series A funding rounds have already developed substantial user bases and have proven to investors that they are prepared for success on a larger scale. Series B funding is used to grow the company so that it can meet these levels of demand.

EHE insight: There are a number of groups and associations (like EHE Group) that have connections to a number of investors that can make the process of finding this type of funding much easier.

Series C funding

Businesses that make it to series C funding sessions are already quite successful. These companies look for additional funding in order to help them develop new products, expand into new markets, or even to acquire other companies. In Series C rounds, investors inject capital into the meat of successful businesses, in an effort to receive more than double that amount back. It can also include follow-on investment from existing investors. Series C funding is focused on scaling the company, growing as quickly and as successfully as possible.

EHE insight: There are a number of groups and associations (like EHE Group) that have connections to a number of investors that can make the process of finding this type of funding much easier.

Shares

There are four main types of shares to be aware of:

- Ordinary shares: they are ordinary if they are not a special type (see below)
- Redeemable shares: these can be repurchased by the company

- Preference shares: these have prior entitlement to payouts
- Alphabet shares: these often appear in CAP Tables and are written as A, B, C etc. They have different rights and priorities attached.

EHE insight: The preference and priority of alphabet shares are the ones investors value the most, because when they have these it means their cash has a priority ranking over other people's cash. Sometimes this is right and other times not. You need to be careful and be aware of what type of shares are allocated and in what priority order (in the case of alphabet shares). This controlling point of risk is worth considering.

Trade sale

This occurs when a company is sold to another operating company which is in the same, or a related, industry or sector.

EHE insight: Selling your company to trade often means you will generate greater shareholder value. The reason being that often a trade buyer will pay more for a competitive advantage and/or will be able to streamline known costs.

Unicorn

A privately held company valued at over £1 billion in the latest funding round.

EHE insight: *More and more investors are looking for companies with the potential to reach "unicorn" level. It's the target for most entrepreneurs too!*

These are the key investor terms. However, for a more complete list of terms you may come across, JP Morgan have a very comprehensive list which can be accessed here: https://am.jpmorgan.com/us/en/asset-management/adv/resources/glossary-of-investment-terms/

ABOUT THE AUTHORS

Pete Evison

Pete is an experienced professional with over 20 years in the tech, software and consulting industries, taking various senior and board level positions.

Before joining the EHE Group, Pete assumed the position of Commercial Director and shareholder at Cake Solutions, overseeing the journey from startup to a multi-million pound turnover company recognised as being at the forefront of open source technologies.

Using his diverse skills and experience, Pete is now channelling his passion into several non-executive roles as well as overseeing the operations for EHE. In addition to his working commitments, Pete loves to wander around the Lake District with his family and brace of Labradors and, weather permitting, also loves to turn his hand to his longest standing passion, fishing.

Ross Faith

Ross has over 25 years' experience, holding several senior executive and non-executive roles supporting owner-managed, family-run organisations through to UK PLC-listed businesses across numerous services and sectors.

His experience has been gained in working with some truly entrepreneurial leaders in helping establish startups, growing their business models quickly and effectively and when things do get tough, to restructure and build again where necessary. He quickly grasps complex situations, analyses possible solutions and delivers cohesive short-, medium – and long-term strategies to deliver required results for all stakeholders.

Having worked with some truly inspirational entrepreneurs, Ross provides an honest assessment of what is needed to be done to support teams in delivering fast sustainable businesses for the future. He loves to support people, teams and focuses on their purpose, wellbeing and drive to make sure they achieve the "best that they can be!"

Gary Fletcher

Gary founded EHE Group in 2021 with Guy whom he has known for over a decade through attending Strategic Coach® Program in Toronto. Gary has transformed many different businesses over the years from sports & leisure facilities to property and tech, ranging from startups to multimillion-pound exits.

As founder and CEO of Forest Holidays, Gary led the growth and transformation from loss making to £10m EBITDA and exited in 2017. Following this success, he has been an investor and Non Exec Chairman of numerous companies all creating significant shareholder value. These roles have supported and guided CEOs/entrepreneurs with private equity backing, fundraising and fast growth.

Gary is also Chairman of the charity KidsVillage.org, which he founded with his daughter. Kids Village aims to build and operate the UK's first magical holiday village just for children with critical illness.

You'll find Gary in a village north of Birmingham with his wife Claire and three daughters, he's also a keen Derby County supporter.

Guy Remond

Guy founded the EHE Group with Gary Fletcher in 2021 with the aim of helping entrepreneurs scale through fast growth through funding and education.

As a founder and non-exec director of thestartupfactory. tech, and co-founder of Cake Solutions (now part of Walt Disney Corporation operating under the Disney Streaming Services brand, building the Disney+ Streaming service), Guy has a passion for technology and entrepreneurship.

With experience in overseeing businesses from small startups to multi-million pound companies, Guy has advised many entrepreneurs and businesses who are looking to achieve ambitious growth targets as well as building two other businesses of his own.

Guy has a keen focus on personal development and culture within organisations, and now turns his hand to various investor and non-exec roles across the commercial sector.

Elliot Smith

Elliot is a qualified accountant and experienced finance professional with over 20 years of experience providing accounting, financial and advisory services to startups, entrepreneurs and established businesses. He works with a variety of entrepreneurial businesses as an advisor, director and investor and his role at the EHE Group involves reviewing and overseeing investments, and working directly with all parties on business strategy, due diligence and deal structuring.

Elliot provides financial and strategic advice, backed up by his many years of commercial, financial and business experience across a wide range of services and sectors. He is an excellent sounding board for entrepreneurs who are looking to secure funding or expand their business, and offers pragmatic advice to help businesses achieve their objectives.

Nyree Trimbel

Nyree has over 15 years' international experience across a range of sectors including travel, education, retail and wellness. She works with a portfolio of businesses and startups, advising them on their marketing and growth strategies, campaign development and channel execution.

With a people – and customer-first mentality, Nyree is passionate about brand building across all sectors, ensuring a business' marketing strategy is aligned to their target market, scalable and, most importantly, delivers commercial results.